THE COMMUNITY COLLEGE BACCALAUREATE

THE COMMUNITY COLLEGE BACCALAUREATE

Emerging Trends and Policy Issues

Deborah L. Floyd

Michael L. Skolnik

Kenneth P. Walker

STERLING, VIRGINIA

COPYRIGHT © 2005 BY

Sty/us

Published by Stylus Publishing, LLC
22883 Quicksilver Drive
Sterling, Virginia 20166-2102

**Library of Congress
Cataloging-in-Publication Data**

ISBN 1-57922-129-7 (cloth)
ISBN 1-57922-130-0 (paper)

Printed in the United States of America

All first editions printed on acid free paper
that meets the American National Standards
Institute
Z39-48 Standard.

First Edition, 2005

10 9 8 7 6 5 4 3 2 1

This book is dedicated to community college students who are benefiting from increased access to baccalaureate degrees due to the advocacy of pathfinders who are working tirelessly and creatively to increase opportunities for access. We hope that this book will serve as a catalyst for conversation about meaningful ways higher education practitioners, researchers, and policy makers can work collaboratively to advocate for increased student access and the democratization of the baccalaureate degree.

Pathfinders and innovators need encouragement and support to build and sustain their momentum of change and development. The Community College Baccalaureate Association and its growing membership in the United States and abroad is gratefully acknowledged as a strong advocate for this movement and for serving an important role as a convener of pathfinders. We are also appreciative of The League for Innovation in the Community Colleges' encouragement to continue this innovation of increasing access to the baccalaureate and to do so for the right reason–students.

We are grateful to our institutions, Florida Atlantic University, The University of Toronto, and Edison College, for providing us the opportunity to prepare this book. And finally, to our families, friends, boards, students, and colleagues who have encouraged us during our passionate journey, we thank you and ask for your continued support as we work collaboratively to continue our research and advocacy about increasing access to the baccalaureate degree for community college students.

Deborah L. Floyd
Florida Atlantic University
Boca Raton, Florida

Michael L. Skolnik
Ontario Institute for Studies in Education of
The University of Toronto
Toronto, Ontario, Canada

Kenneth P. Walker
Edison College
Fort Myers, Florida

CONTENTS

FOREWORD

Mark David Milliron

Working at a place like the League for Innovation in the Community College provides an interesting view. From our tower stand on the beach, we see wave after wave of innovations and transformations come to shore. However, what is often a beautiful sight from our perch is for you—who stand in the surf—a drenching wave of change that makes it difficult to keep your balance. Given this salty situation, we are cautionary about hyperbole and champions of what we often call in our leadership programs, "reality therapy."

So, it is time to explore the community college baccalaureate, and this book promises an impressive and realistic view. The authors take pains to offer a balanced look at this innovative and transformative wave. Michael L. Skolnik, Deborah L. Floyd, Kenneth P. Walker, and the host of thoughtful and thorough scholars and practitioners outline the policy and practice issues and their implications with great candor. More importantly, they provide a range of quality examples to benchmark and compelling political realities to ponder. The following chapters will provide you with a solid look at both the beauty and furor of what seems to be a rising tide; but, keep in mind that this is likely part of a larger wave, and not just an idiosyncratic innovation.

In *Feels like Third Wave: The Rise of Fundraising in the Community College* (Milliron, de los Santos, & Browning, 2004), we tried to put the explosive interest in private fundraising in the larger context of three significant waves of innovation that swept ashore in the last hundred years. First was *comprehensive integration* and the push to bring together the worlds of the junior college and technical institutes—academic and vocational education—an effort that dominated the 1960s and 1970s and, for some, stands as a fundamental issue today. This first wave signaled the beginnings of the comprehensive community college. Next, we outlined the rise of *entrepreneurial expansion* and the tide of work-force development activities and corporate training that flowed through the 1980s and 1990s, pushed on by the quality movement and the information technology revolution. This second wave brought our institutions into the light as essential community learning and training partners. It also raised our political influence. Finally, we argued that the rise of fundraising in the community college was part of a larger third transformation wave of *institutional advancement* that is forming, foaming, frothing, and already flooding across our movement. The swell of institutional advancement signals the entry of our institutions as full partners on the economic and educational horizon, necessitating the advancement of programming and resources.

Each of these waves had profound implications for internal operations, external relations, and the adoption of best practices. For example, internally, we had to literally merge institutions in the first wave, adopt more business practices in the second, and restructure our foundations in the third. Externally, we had to rename our colleges, wrestle for noncredit funding, and create new pricing systems in the second surge. We had to make our case for our evolving role in the third. In terms of best-practice adoption, the League for Innovation was a child of the first wave, helped lead the best-practice adoption of the second, and is swimming fast and furiously along with the third.

The community college baccalaureate clearly is part of the confluence of the third wave. As our institutions advance in function, form, and fundraising, the ability to create pathways to, and sometimes provide the core access for, the baccalaureate seems a natural part of the evolutionary flow. But it doesn't mean that it's going to be easy, as the authors here make clear. You can't "just do it!"

Even so, when asked to speak to the inaugural Community College Baccalaureate Association Conference, I presented a "Just Do It" message. However, I argued that if we are going to ride this wave, we have to *just do it for the right reasons*. We have to be honest about our expansion of baccalaureate options and make sure that these moves are about service-area need, not executive or faculty ego. Also, we should *just do it the community college way;* which means we should strive to continue our commitment to being good partners, being creative, and ensuring our values. This is particularly important in regard to our commitment to open-access issues and developmental education. It would be a sad irony if democracy's colleges become more exclusive enclaves of education. Finally, we should *just do it thoughtfully*. All too often, the argument for the community college baccalaureate (and other innovations as well) is predicated on bashing other sectors of education. We have to be careful to respect the distinct roles we all play in the education world. For example, we should not publicly punish research universities for doing research. This conduct is the equivalent of them bashing us for *not* doing research. In addition, we have to be thoughtful about the host of internal cultural issues that emerge. Differential faculty loads and facility needs are just the tip of the cultural challenge pyramid in this landscape. And finally, we have to be careful not to adopt the arrogance that all too often creeps into higher education. We are bastions of open access and community care. Arrogance because of our expanding role could easily become an Achilles' heel.

With all of this said, I now encourage you to join the authors here and dive into the surf. Riding any wave takes patience. We have to get our board ready and paddle out a bit. We have to learn to get up on the board and keep our balance. We have to be ready for unexpected surges and sudden crosscurrents. And let's not mention the sharks. Just keep in mind that the courage necessary to ride this wave is in full relief every day in the students who have made the bold choice to dive into your educational programs and change their lives.

Reference

Milliron, M., de los Santos, G., & Browning, B. (2004). "Feels like third wave: The rise of fundraising in the community college." In M. Milliron, G. de los Santos, & B. Browning (Eds.), *Successful Approaches to Fundraising and Development. New Directions for Community Colleges*, *124*, 81–94. San Francisco: Jossey-Bass.

1

PERSPECTIVES ON THE COMMUNITY COLLEGE BACCALAUREATE

Deborah L. Floyd
and Michael L. Skolnik

Traditionally, community colleges confer degrees and offer programs that are less than four years in duration. These colleges have been called "people's colleges," primarily because of their open-access admissions policies, their affordable costs, and their geographic locations that are within easy driving distance for most people.

During the past few years, however, community college leaders, policy makers, and legislators have been seriously exploring—and, in some states and Canadian provinces, implementing—the notion of community colleges offering and conferring bachelor's degrees, especially in certain high-need areas as teacher education and nursing (Floyd and Walker, 2003; Cook, 2000; Evelyn, 2002 and 2003; Skolnik, 2001). Some leaders see these changes as a natural extension of the evolution of the community college focus on access (Walker, 2000 and 2001; Garmon, 2003; McKinney, 2003), while others view the awarding of the community college baccalaureate degrees as inappropriate and as a threat to the basic core values of this unique sector of higher education (Mills, 2003; Lane, 2003; Townsend as cited by Troumpoucis, 2004; Wattenbarger, 2000).

The focus of this book is to describe the emerging trend on the part of community colleges in conferring baccalaureate degrees, in both the United States and Canada. In an effort to contribute to the development of policy in this area, most authors identify important policy issues and research challenges.

This topic is very significant to higher education because the very fabric of the traditional community college mission is being challenged by the addition of baccalaureate degree programs. Most recently, community colleges in states such as Utah, Nevada, Arkansas, Florida, and Texas have been authorized by state governing bodies to confer baccalaureate degrees. Other states, such as South Carolina, Maryland, and Arizona have noted some legislative activity directly relevant to this issue.

Institutions that retain the basic mission of a community college while beginning to confer some baccalaureate degrees may be considered hybrid institutions. Such colleges may pose problems for regional and national accrediting agencies and for classification systems, such as the Carnegie Classification of Institutions of Higher Education.

Understandably, some university leaders are concerned about this trend because the awarding of bachelor's degrees by community colleges is often viewed as a threat to the undergraduate mission of universities. These and other criticisms of the community college baccalaureate degree will be discussed in various chapters and emphasized in Chapter 11 by Barbara K. Townsend.

This expanded role for community colleges is not limited to the United States. In Canada, more than a quarter of community colleges now offer baccalaureate programs; and debates, similar to those in the United States on this issue, are occurring in Canada, as described in Chapter 4 by Michael L. Skolnik.

This is a hot and somewhat controversial topic, not only among community college and university leadership, but also among politicians, business leaders, students, and policy makers; all of whom are concerned with addressing issues of access, costs, relevant curricular needs, and purposes of postsecondary education.

Why did we prepare this book? First, we wanted to describe, document, and—insofar as possible—understand what appears to be a very significant development in postsecondary education. Second, we wanted this book to be a catalyst for conversation, to help stimulate public dialogue within a consistent framework of terminology, and to encourage others to research and write about this percolating movement. Third, recognizing that there has been a lot of polarization around this issue, we hoped that one outcome of producing this book would be a more informed understanding of these diverse views, resulting in a greater recognition of common ground among stakeholders; for example, as a direct result of the conversations that were part of preparing this book, the Community College Baccalaureate Association expanded its mission to embrace diverse models of delivery, beyond those in which the community college confers the degree. Finally, we felt that preparing this book would afford us an opportunity to contribute to the ongoing reflection about the mission, values, and purpose of the community college, now and in the future.

This book attempts to focus on manuscripts from practitioners and scholars in an effort to describe the movement through stories of programs and practices, while challenging readers to embrace the policy and research opportunities for the future. The book is loosely organized in sections. The first chapters focus on the history and rationale for the movement, and include an overview of models and programs in the United States and Canada. The next set of chapters, which are very practitioner oriented, describe specific institutional   and in one case province-wide—initiatives for developing and implementing community college baccalaureate programs. The last set of chapters are an eclectic group that address the issues of critics, summarize major themes for policy and research for the future, and provide resources for further exploration of this topic.

In addition to describing the rationale for development of the community college baccalaureate, in Chapter 2, Kenneth P. Walker documents the founding and activities of the Community College Baccalaureate Association (CCBA). As the founder of the CCBA, Walker offers a strong case for support of the community college baccalaureate.

In Chapter 3, Deborah L. Floyd describes models of delivery of baccalaureate programming in the United States and offers a four-part typology of community college and related baccalaureate degrees. She differentiates between models of articulation, university center, university extension and the community college baccalaureate in describing relevant developments across the United States. This chapter, like the ones that follow, identifies a number of issues for policy and challenges for research.

In Chapter 4, Michael L. Skolnik traces the development of community college baccalaureate programming in Canada from the late

1980s to the present. This chapter describes how the community college baccalaureate has been used by provincial governments to make systems of higher education more responsive to labor market and other societal needs. Recognizing that the applied baccalaureate has been the predominant model in Canada, this chapter provides detail on the standards and procedures for approval of applied baccalaureates in Alberta and Ontario.

One of the most popular approaches to the delivery of the baccalaureate in community college service areas is the university center approach. In this model, community colleges do not confer baccalaureate degrees themselves, but work collaboratively to deliver them in cooperation with universities. In Chapter 5, Albert L. Lorenzo describes six distinct university center models and gives examples of each. These models are: co-location, enterprise, virtual, integrated, sponsorship, and hybrid. He identifies factors that contribute to successful implementation of university centers.

One of the reasons many states have supported the idea of the community college baccalaureate is to address identified and unmet workforce needs. In Chapter 6, Kenneth P. Walker and Deborah L. Floyd offer a rationale for the community college to offer applied workforce baccalaureate degrees and provide several examples of applied workforce baccalaureate programs in different states.

St. Petersburg College was the first community college in Florida authorized to confer baccalaureate degrees. In Chapter 7, Thomas Furlong describes the intricate processes for approval, accreditation, curriculum development, and other pragmatic aspects of implementing new baccalaureate programs. He offers practical suggestions and advice about lessons learned that may be useful to others who are considering adding baccalaureate degrees to their offerings.

In Chapter 8, Jonathon V. McKee describes the 1998 development of the first baccalaureate program at Westark College, the Bachelor of Manufacturing Technology degree, designed to address the workforce needs of the Fort Smith, Arkansas region. He discusses the curricular aspects of this program, including integration of general education and industry-specific competencies into student-centered, self-paced competency models. In 2002, Westark College's name and governance structure were changed, and the institution is now the University of Arkansas at Fort Smith.

Located in rural Nevada, Great Basin College was approved to offer a baccalaureate degree in elementary education in 1999. In Chapter 9, Ron and Nancy Remington relate the chronological details pertaining to the development, accreditation, funding, and actual implementation of this new baccalaureate degree. Based on their experiences, they provide a candid discussion of the lessons learned.

In Chapter 10, Berta Vigil Laden reports on a field-based study that she conducted of applied baccalaureate degrees in Ontario, Canada. In that study, she examined the perceptions of administrators and faculty in the Ontario colleges regarding these new degree programs and the impact that they have had on the institutions.

Although the community college baccalaureate has many advocates and supporters, there are also many within the community college sector who fear this movement may have some undesirable consequences, or who at least believe that considerable caution should accompany any move toward the conferring of baccalaureate degrees by community colleges. In Chapter 11, Barbara K. Townsend analyzes opinions of those for and against community college baccalaureates and offers her own perspective on how these new degrees may impact community colleges in general. She offers thoughtful comments about research challenges and policy issues.

In Chapter 12, we identify major conceptual features of the community college baccalaureate as it has been developing, summarize key policy issues, and indicate important research needs. We discuss how the community college baccalaureate program affects the way the community college sees itself and the way it is seen by others. We also speculate why this development has generated so much interest, not just in the United States and Canada, but in other countries as well.

One of the challenges for those who want to learn more about the community college baccalaureate movement has been the limited resources and literature on the topic. Chapter 13 by Michelle Eastham offers a compilation of U.S. and Canadian resources such as Web sites, journal articles, trade news articles, conference papers, books, and chapters that relate directly or indirectly to this topic. We hope that this resource section will be useful to practitioners, policy leaders, and researchers who want to know more about this emerging trend.

Finally, prior to the index, brief biographical descriptions of the authors and editors are included. Our authors are an impressive group of practitioners and scholars who have been pathfinders in this emerging area. We are grateful to each of these professionals for the time they devoted to research and writing, and most importantly, for their patience and persistence in dealing with our numerous editorial recommendations.

One of the challenges of edited books like this is the potential for overlap among chapters. Although we have attempted to limit the amount of overlap, the case and thematic focus of many chapters necessitate that some of same facts and issues be discussed, even if from different perspectives.

Another challenge is keeping current with the shifts and changes associated with community colleges receiving authorization and accreditation for these new baccalaureate degree programs and implementing them. If the past is a reflection of the future, we know that some of the specific examples and facts cited in this book will soon become dated. We have done our best to ensure the information presented here is as accurate as possible, at least at press time, knowing that this book offers only a snapshot of history in the making, as community colleges continue to change and evolve.

A delightful outcome of our processes as we prepared this book has been the opportunity for Canadian and U.S. community college professionals to work together as colleagues and to learn from each other. The community colleges in our two countries have much in common, but enough that is different to offer stimulating opportunities for further collaborative ventures.

References

Cook, A. (2000). *Community college baccalaureate degrees: A delivery model for the future?* Policy paper. Denver, CO: Education Commission of the States.

Evelyn, J. (March 8, 2002). States give community colleges a role in educating teachers. *The Chronicle of Higher Education.* A 22–23.

Evelyn, J. (April 11, 2003). Making waves in Miami: A leading community college offers bachelor's degrees, reflecting national tension between 2- and 4-year sectors. *The Chronicle of Higher Education.* A 34–35.

Floyd, D. L., & Walker, D. A. (2003). Community college teacher education: A typology, challenging issues and state views. *Community College Journal of Research and Practice, 27*(8), 643–663.

Garmon, J. (April 14, 2003). Closing the degree divide. *Community College Week, 15*(18), 4–5.

Lane, K. (April 14, 2003). 2 + 2 = ? *Community College Week, 15*(18), 6–8.

McKinney, D. T. (April 14, 2003). We need the baccalaureate now. *Community College Week, 15*(18), 4.

Mills, K. (Fall, 2003). Community college baccalaureates: Some critics decry the trend as "mission creep." *National CrossTalk.* The National Center for Public Policy and Higher Education.

Skolnik, M. L. (2001). *The community college baccalaureate: Its meaning and implications for the organization of postsecondary education, the mission and character of the community college and the bachelor's degree.* Unpublished paper delivered at the First Annual Community College Baccalaureate Association Conference, Orlando, Florida, February 7–9, 2001.

Troumpoucis, P. (April 12, 2004). The best of both worlds? *Community College Week, 16*(16), 6–8.

Walker, K. P. (February, 2000). The workforce bachelor's degree. *The Education Digest, 65,* 61–66.

Walker, K. P. (April, 2001). An open door to the bachelor's degree. *Leadership Abstracts.* The League for Innovation in the Community College.

Wattenbarger, J. (2000). Colleges should stick to what they do best. *Community College Week, 13*(18), 4–5.

2

HISTORY, RATIONALE, AND THE COMMUNITY COLLEGE BACCALAUREATE ASSOCIATION

Kenneth P. Walker[1]

The first section of this chapter looks briefly at the evolution of higher education in the United States. The second section considers the rationale underlying the introduction and implementation of the community college baccalaureate. The third summarizes the fast pace of developments since 1997, including the emergence of the Community College Baccalaureate Association, a new international organization dedicated to advocacy for access to the baccalaureate. The chapter finishes with some policy recommendations and avenues for future research.

History

Early Colleges

Education has been important to American society from the first European colonization of North America to the twenty-first century. The colonists in New Netherland did not want their children to forget the

---

[1] The author thanks and gratefully acknowledges the assistance of Ms. Laurie McDowell, District Director of the Edison University Center, Edison College District, Ft. Myers Florida. She assisted with the preparation of the section about the Community College Baccalaureate Association.

decency and order of a civilized life. So, in 1649, the Nine Tribunes wrote to the States General in Holland about "the sad state into which learning had fallen in the colony and recommended a public school . . . so that the youth be well instructed, not only in reading and writing, but also in the knowledge and fear of the Lord" (Wright, 1957, p. 105).

Even vocational versus academic learning was a matter of disagreement and debate during early colonial times. William Penn was an "early advocate of adapting schools to the practical needs of humanity instead of slavishly following outworn methods" (Wright, 1957, p. 107). Pennsylvania emphasized practical over classical education.

Higher education in the colonies started at Harvard College in Cambridge, Massachusetts, in 1636. The preparation of ministers spurred establishment of many early colleges. In addition, such institutions provided instruction in the trivium (i.e., grammar, rhetoric, and logic) and the quadrivium (i.e., arithmetic, music, geometry, and astronomy). Colonists eager to prepare ministers and provide education comparable to that in England, established the College of William and Mary in Williamsburg, Virginia, in 1693 by British royal charter, and the Collegiate School in New Haven, Connecticut, in 1701, renamed Yale in 1718 for an early benefactor. Other than at seminaries, there was little academic training in the professions before 1763. Attorneys and doctors who were not able to travel to England for studies learned their trades through apprenticeships (Wright, 1957).

A pattern of evolution and change has characterized higher education in the United States throughout its history. The early colleges no longer primarily prepare ministers. Vertical expansion of college programs (so-called mission creep) has resulted in comprehensive universities. Some universities even offer certificates of completion and associate degrees. So, one might ask, what is the point of all this? The answer is simple: Community colleges, as well as all other colleges, evolve their missions and adapt their programs and services vertically to respond to changing needs in the communities that they serve. What is traditional today was not traditional 200, or even 50 years ago. There have been dramatic changes in who is educated and how they are educated.

Junior Colleges

In 1901, the first of a new type of college opened in Joliet, Illinois. This junior college was to provide access to college for poorly prepared students (Cohen & Brawer, 1996). U.S. society and the economy were based first on agriculture, then on industry, and today on information and knowledge. As society has evolved, so has education in response. It is again essential to expand educational opportunity to everyone in today's knowledge-based society. Just as community colleges democratized higher education through their open-door philosophy and associate degrees, so they must now democratize opportunity for higher education through the baccalaureate degree. Community colleges must not condone those who would, under the guise of maintaining quality and controlling competition, restrict access to higher education.

Higher Education for American Democracy (the Truman Commission Report) in 1947 called for a major expansion of education services. It proposed encouraging and enabling all Americans to explore their full educational potential, stating that "The American people should set as their ultimate goal an educational system in which at no level . . . will a qualified individual . . . encounter an economic barrier to the attainment of the kind of education suited to his aptitudes and interests" (Witt, Wattenbarger, Gollattscheck, & Suppiger, 1994, p. 131).

The commission suggested the name "community college" for colleges designed chiefly to serve local educational needs. "And it noted that it may have various forms of organization and may have curricula of various lengths. Its dominant feature is its intimate relations to the life of the community it serves" (Witt et al., 1994, p. 131). "The community college seeks to become the center of learning for the entire community. . . . It gears its programs and services to the needs and wishes of the people it serves" (Witt et al., 1994, p. 132).

Nowhere does the report limit community colleges to two-year programs; open-door access and responsiveness to community needs are to be their primary values. If community colleges are to be true to these fundamental values, they must respond anytime there is an identified need in the communities that they serve, including one for baccalaureate degrees. As Edmund Gleazer, Jr. has stated, "[t]he basic, inexorable, unmistakable fact and force to deal with is that of CHANGE—unparalleled and unprecedented change that perplexes the public, confounds the authorities, and demands response from education, one of its instigators" (1980, p. 2). Gleazer went on to say that "[t]he institution must be able to change as communities change with new conditions, demands, or circumstances" (pp. 4–5).

We build our present and future on the wisdom of scholars and leaders from earlier generations. We can measure a proposition's enduring value by the extent to which it remains relevant. Truly great minds live in the present and envision the future. Thus, the Truman Report and Gleazer were prophetic. The values that guided the junior colleges are relevant today even as community colleges consider offering bachelor's degrees.

Beginnings of the Community College Baccalaureate Degree

It is difficult to identify the first instance in which a community college offered the baccalaureate. Throughout the twentieth century it was not uncommon for a junior college to evolve into a four-year college. What began to happen in the 1980s, and more particularly in the late 1990s, was for some community colleges to decide to offer a few baccalaureate programs in selected areas in order to provide access to baccalaureate for students who would not otherwise be able to earn a four-year degree. In most cases, these contemporary community colleges have stated that their goal was to maintain emphasis on traditional community college values while at the same time adding baccalaureate programs that complemented their emphasis on access.

For instance, in 1985, Navarro College in Texas sought legislative approval to offer baccalaureate degrees.[2] Later, in 1993, Utah Valley Community College received legislative approval to offer baccalaureate degrees and in 1997, the Arkansas legislature authorized Westark Community College to develop a bachelor's degree in manufacturing technology. In 1999, the Utah legislature authorized Dixie State College to offer a bachelor's degree in education. In 1999, Great Basin College

---

[2] The author was president of Navarro College during this time. The bill, which did not leave committee, was authored by Tom Waldrop, a Texas state representative.

in Reno, Nevada began offering a bachelor's degree in education. Colleges in Arizona, Kansas, and Oregon have unsuccessfully sought approval to offer baccalaureate degrees. The Florida Council of Community College presidents endorsed community colleges offering selected baccalaureate degrees in 1997[3] and later, in 2001, the Florida legislature greatly expanded the authority of the state's community colleges to offer four-year degrees.

The Florida legislation expands access to baccalaureate programs through community colleges; authorizes these institutions to offer a few baccalaureates to meet local workforce needs; prohibits them from terminating programs for associate in arts or associate in science degrees; and reinforces their primary mission as provider of associate degrees.

Very recently, in 2003, Texas and Hawaii authorized some community colleges in their states to add baccalaureate programs. In Chapter 3, Deborah L. Floyd describes these and other developments pertaining to the community college baccalaureate in the United States. From the increase in the number of states and colleges that have shown interest in the community college baccalaureate, especially since the 1990s, it is clear that the momentum for community colleges providing baccalaureate access has accelerated.

Rationale

The rationale for community colleges to add baccalaureate degrees to their offerings can be explained from both a societal perspective and an institutional perspective. From a societal perspective, a key factor is meeting the need for a baccalaureate educated workforce. Insofar as community college students experience barriers which limit baccalaureate attainment, the opportunity for them to complete their baccalaureate at the community college could likely increase their income and their contributions to society. From an institutional perspective, an issue for the community college is that many of the occupations for

---

[3] The author introduced the resolution of support to the Florida Community College presidents and it passed by a vote of twenty to one. (Florida Council of Presidents minutes, September, 1997.) Thomas Furlong, in Chapter 7, further describes the legislation and evolution of baccalaureate authorization in Florida.

which it has been providing education have, in recent years, elevated their entry requirements to the baccalaureate level. Thus, if the community college is to continue to be a major provider of graduates for these occupations it is necessary for the community college to ensure that students in these programs have the opportunity to obtain the necessary credential—a baccalaureate. In Chapter 3, a variety of models for doing this will be discussed, including the direct provision of the baccalaureate by community colleges.

Interest in the community college baccalaureate is in response to a variety of social and economic concerns. Three factors affect the motivation for community colleges to offer baccalaureate degrees: rising demand of employers and students, rising costs of universities, and limited programs and access to meet these demands. How will community colleges change to address these challenges, especially when students are demanding more access to opportunities for the bachelor's degree?

Community colleges are being confronted with competition from a variety of educational providers. Challenges to their survival will come from charter colleges, e-colleges, broker colleges, proprietary colleges, and private nonprofit institutions granting baccalaureate degrees. To be competitive, community colleges must develop new products and delivery systems, and shed the confining title of "two-year college."

The nation's social and economic foundations are at risk because more education is needed for productive employment, and access to college is being denied to millions of students (Commission on National Investment in Higher Education, 1997).

The national crisis in higher education calls for creative solutions. Traditional thinking, based on past experiences and limited by defensiveness and personal interests, does a disservice to the millions of students who need baccalaureate degrees, but who cannot attend a university. Community colleges can develop innovative ways to address rising demand, limited access, and increasing costs. If it is true that "widespread access to higher education . . . is critical to the economic health and social welfare of the nation" (Commission on National Investment in Higher Education, 1997, p. 2), community colleges must play a major role in the delivery of those degrees.

The facilities, faculty, staff, and programs are already in place at conveniently located community colleges across the nation. Expanding missions to include baccalaureate degrees without changing the open-door philosophy is a logical option. Missions should not reflect a bygone era, but rather respond, adapt, and grow in ways appropriate to changing communities.

The market for higher education is increasingly consumer driven, and it has become international in scope. The Internet enables colleges and universities to enroll students from anywhere in the world. Competition is increasing rapidly from private nonprofit and private for-profit institutions that now award degrees. There were 400 U.S. corporate universities in 1988, and there are more than 1,000 today (Meister, 1998), many of them now accredited by regional associations.

Such private competitors may transform higher education. According to the *Chronicle of Higher Education*, lawmakers and business leaders warned the annual meeting of the Education Commission of the States that "more and more companies are creating their own colleges or asking for-profit institutions like the University of Phoenix to train their employees because public colleges are too slow to respond to the corporations' needs" (Selingo & Basinger, 1999, p. A61). Business leaders also said that for-profit institutions have cutting-edge programs and move students through more quickly (Selingo & Basinger, 1999).

The three Cs—competition, cooperation, and collaboration—are becoming forces in the decision-making process for higher education. University centers and collaborative efforts between community colleges and universities have emerged on community college campuses across the country. Examples are Macomb Community College in Michigan; North Harris Montgomery Community College in Texas; and St. Petersburg College and Edison College in Florida. In addition, the Open University in Britain is exploring partnerships with community colleges to make baccalaureate degrees available through distance learning. In Chapter 5, Al Lorenzo examines some of these university center models.

Given heightened demand and growing competition, the colleges that attract students will be those that best adapt to change. To remain relevant, community colleges must prepare to do new things and not simply do the same things differently. It is time for them to rethink their *raisons d'etre* and to assess the current competition. The complexities of the modern world require community colleges to adapt their services and forge a plan that should include the baccalaureate degree.

As student demand for the baccalaureate increases, community colleges have the capacity to accommodate this demand. Performing this role is a natural progression in the evolution of the mission of the community college.

A number of factors are reshaping higher education and have significant implications for the role of the community college with regard to the baccalaureate:

- The market has become international.
- A large proportion of students are older part-timers and are working.
- The baccalaureate is replacing the associate degree as the entry-level credential for many jobs that pay the best salaries and offer opportunities for promotions.
- The Internet has changed service area boundaries and resulted in a wide variety of new providers of baccalaureate programs.

In an age that places a premium on intellectual capital, a nation that fails to maintain first-rate education risks losing its economic and social position. Community colleges help to ensure that a nation's workforce remains globally competitive by addressing the rising demand for, limited access to, and increasing costs of baccalaureate education.

Distinctive Strengths

Widespread access to higher education is critical to the economic health and social welfare of any nation. Community colleges must expand their role in providing this access by offering baccalaureate degrees. By doing so, they will help promote the following:

- increased geographical, financial, and academic access to higher education;

- cost efficiencies through existing infrastructure;

- success among nontraditional or returning students through smaller classes, less-rigid sequencing, and greater scheduling options;

- ready matriculation and upward mobility for students with associate degrees;

- stable family and employment relationships for students while they complete their degrees;

- community college commitment to economic and workforce development; and

- responsiveness to community needs for specialized programs.

Community colleges are uniquely qualified to train and educate a workforce to the level necessary to meet future needs. Moreover, with their history of serving disadvantaged and minority students, they can open the door to greater access. Offering the baccalaureate is a logical next step—the community college can provide it to more learners, at convenient locations, in a more learner-centered environment, and at greatly reduced cost.

Increased demand for higher education is challenging community colleges. "Projected increases in the number of college-age students threaten to overwhelm many state public higher education systems during the next decade" (Ehrenberg, 2000, p. 34). Community colleges were designed to serve students not readily admissible to university because of limited financial means, poor academic records, language difficulties, or family concerns. They continue to serve those students well and to adapt and adjust their programs. Surveys and focus groups show that students, in addition to needing basic skills and short-cycle training and certification, want baccalaureate degrees. Transfer to traditional colleges or universities may not be suitable for them, and they would like to earn their bachelor's degree at their local community college.

Demographics may be an underlying force for change. Community college student demographics often mirror the communities they serve and they are becoming increasingly diverse. Having found success at the community college, more students want to pursue the baccalaureate and would prefer to do so locally in their communities. Community college leaders are fiercely loyal to these nontraditional students, and some ask: "Why we should give these students two years of education and then say, 'we can't serve you anymore—you're on your own—go to a university if you can afford it, and if you can overcome the obstacles that are in your way.'"

Facing the Critics

It is often said that students who start at a community college are significantly less likely to complete a four-year degree than students who begin at a four-year college or university. Completion rates at community colleges are elusive; many students do not seek a degree, much less pursue upper-division studies. In Florida, however, degree-seeking community college students in the upper division of the state university system traditionally do as well as or better than people who enroll there as freshmen (Florida Community College System, 1999). Indeed, permitting community colleges to offer selected baccalaureates could enhance access rates by making upper-division studies accessible to more students.

Critics argue that granting higher degrees implies an abandonment of the community college mission. According to Wattenbarger, "It would be difficult, if not impossible, to convince anyone that the bachelor's degree offered by a community college is as important as the one offered by a university or a four-year college" (Wattenbarger, 2000, p. 4). However, the regional accrediting associations hold such community colleges to the same standards as universities, so this criticism is questionable. Surely the quality of degrees varies among universities, so it could also be argued that degrees from some universities are not as respected as those from other universities. Adding the baccalaureate to the mission of the community college is not shifting focus; it is adding a focus in order to increase relevance. What proponents are saying is, "Keep the core values of the community colleges," and to the students, "We are not going to get you halfway there and then abandon you. We are going to take you all the way to the baccalaureate degree."

Future Directions: Building on Strengths

It is possible that students might pay less tuition for a baccalaureate at a community college than at a state university. Lower costs and convenient locations would increase opportunities for place-bound students, for whom community colleges may offer the only route to a bachelor's degree.

The rising cost of higher education is preventing many students from attaining a bachelor's degree. According to Chris Simmons, assistant director of government relations at the American Council of Education, low-income students remain underrepresented in college compared with middle- and upper-income students (Lane, 2003). Since community colleges enroll a large proportion of low- and moderate-income students, an obvious solution would be to authorize community colleges to confer baccalaureates. The infrastructure is already in place and adding two more years of education would be far less costly than building new universities.

Community colleges have played a major role in the higher education revolution of the twentieth century. Some educators believe that the revolution is almost over. "Two years of postsecondary education are within the reach—financially, geographically, practically—of virtually every American. . . . Open-admission policies and programs for everyone ensure that no member of the community need miss the chance to attend" (Cohen & Brawer, 1996, p. 31).

If associate degrees were enough to gain good jobs and advance in careers, then perhaps the revolution would be almost over. In the competition for the best jobs, however, the baccalaureate is an essential credential. Just as community colleges democratized access to the associate degree, they must now do the same for the baccalaureate. Education opens the door to success, and every person should have an equal opportunity to pursue the bachelor's degree at a minimum.

Whereas addition of the baccalaureate will change community colleges, there is no reason why their core values of open-door access, learner-centeredness, affordability, convenience, and responsiveness could not be maintained. Granting the bachelor's degree will take community colleges out of the undesirable position of offering "incomplete" education and transform them from halfway colleges on the way to a baccalaureate. With this transformation, community colleges could achieve recognition and respect for the quality that they have always provided. The beneficiaries would be the millions of students who would be able to gain more affordable access to a baccalaureate degree.

The Community College Baccalaureate Association

In the late 1990s, it became very apparent to the author that an organization was needed to serve as a convener and catalyst for the growing number of community college practitioners who were concerned about, and wanted to address, these challenges of baccalaureate access in their communities. Thus, The Community College Baccalaureate Association (CCBA) was founded in August, 1999 as a nonprofit organization to promote the development and acceptance of community college baccalaureate degrees as a means of addressing the national problems of student access, demand, and cost; to chronicle further progress in this arena; and to share information and facilitate networking. Florida incorporated the CCBA as a nonprofit organization on June 5, 2000, (CCBA, 2000).

Since its inception, the CCBA has served as a resource center, disseminating articles written by proponents, publishing and distributing a newsletter, and holding annual conferences. Information is available at www.accbd.org, such as articles with theoretical arguments for the community college baccalaureate. At present, CCBA's 130 members represent twenty-eight U.S. states, four Canadian provinces, Bermuda, and Jamaica, as well as research institutions, higher-education governing bodies, and private industry.

The CCBA's first annual conference was held in 2001 in Orlando, Florida, and there have been annual conferences with continually increased attendance. These conferences have featured presentations from practitioners, community college researchers, policy leaders, and others who are interested in issues of access to the baccalaureate. At the most recent conference in 2004, more than sixty institutions from the United States, Canada and other nations were represented.

It is important to note that when the CCBA was founded, its focus was exclusively on advocating for bachelor's degrees developed and awarded by community colleges. In 2004, however, the focus was expanded to include other models of enhancing baccalaureate access including those described in Chapter 3.

The current vision, philosophy, purpose, and mission of the Community College Baccalaureate Association are as follows:

Vision: To be a catalyst for increasing access to the baccalaureate degree at community colleges.

Philosophy: An educated populace is the foundation of a free and prosperous society. The baccalaureate degree is an important entry requirement for the better jobs and a better lifestyle. Therefore, every person should have an opportunity to pursue the baccalaureate degree at a place that is convenient, accessible, and affordable.

Purpose: To promote better access to the baccalaureate degree on community college campuses, and to serve as a resource for information on various models for accomplishing this purpose.

Mission: The purpose will be achieved by:

1. encouraging research, fostering dialogue, and sharing research data, publications, best practices, state legislation, and policies;

2. encouraging development of baccalaureate degrees conferred by community colleges;

3. encouraging development of university centers on community college campuses; and

4. encouraging joint degree programs with universities on community college campuses (CCBA, n.d.).

Clearly, the Community College Baccalaureate Association is meeting a need of community colleges in various countries that are addressing issues of providing baccalaureate programming through various models of delivery. Additional information about the Community College Baccalaureate Association—including conference papers, publications, and other activities of the CCBA—is provided in Chapter 13.

Issues for Research and Policy: Commentary

The purpose of this chapter has been to briefly describe the development of the community college baccalaureate within the context of the historical development of community colleges, to present a rationale or case for support of the community college baccalaureate, and to describe the Community College Baccalaureate Association. A great many issues for policy and research have arisen related to the community college baccalaureate and they are aptly identified and described in the following chapters of this book.

The time has come to stop defining the community college as a two-year institution. Community colleges thrived in the last century because they were the hallmark of change and adaptation while they also remained responsive to their communities and core values. Community colleges should continue to lift the aspirations of ordinary people beyond two years of education and thus, the time is right for a new vision for community colleges, one that embraces a strong commitment to baccalaureate access.

In adding the baccalaureate to their mission, community colleges should heed the advice of Mark Milliron, President and Chief Executive Officer of the League for Innovation in the Community College. In his keynote address to the 2002 annual conference of the Community College Baccalaureate Association, he advised the audience to "be honest about whether you're ready to do this." He added, "do it for the right reasons, do it the community college way, and do it thoughtfully" (Milliron, 2002).

References

Cohen, A. M., & Brawer, F. B. (1996). *The American community college.* 3rd edition. San Francisco: Jossey-Bass, Inc.

Commission on National Investment in Higher Education (J. L. Dionne & T. Kean, Co-Chairs). (1997). Breaking the social contract: The fiscal crisis in higher education. Santa Monica, CA: Council for Aid to Education and Rand Corporation.

Community College Baccalaureate Association (CCBA). (June 5, 2000). Articles of incorporation. Florida Department of State Document No. N00000003823.

Community College Baccalaureate Association. (n.d.). Board of directors. Retrieved August 21, 2003, from www.accbd.org/boardofdirectors.html

Ehrenberg, R. G. (2000). Financial forecasts for the next decade. *Presidency.* Washington, DC: American Council on Education, 34.

Florida Community College System (April 1999). Articulation report. Tallahassee, FL: Florida Board of Education.

Florida Council of Presidents for Community Colleges (September 25–26, 1997). Minutes of meeting, 5.

Gleazer, E. J., Jr. (1980). *The community college: Values, vision, and vitality.* Washington, DC: Community College Press.

Lane, K. (September 1, 2003). Federal withholding. *Community College Week*, 7.

Meister, J. C. (1998). *Corporate universities: Lessons in building a world-class workforce.* New York: McGraw Hill.

Milliron, M. D. (March 17, 2002). Keynote address. Given at the Community College Baccalaureate Association Annual Conference, Boston.

Selingo, J., & Basinger, J. (July 23, 1999). At a meeting, education leaders talk of teacher quality and businesses' needs. *Chronicle of Education, 45*, A61.

Walker, K., & Zeiss, P. A. (December 2000/January 2001). Designs for change: Degrees and skills, baccalaureate degrees and skills certification. *Community College Journal, 71*, 8, 10.

Wattenbarger, J. (2000). Colleges should stick to what they do best. *Community College Week, 13*(18), p. 4–5.

Witt, A. A., Wattenbarger, J. L., Gollattscheck, J. F., & Suppiger, J. E. (1994). *America's community colleges: The first century.* Washington, DC: Community College Press.

Wright, L. B. (1957). *The cultural life of the American colonies.* New York: Harper and Brothers.

3

THE COMMUNITY COLLEGE
BACCALAUREATE IN THE U.S.

MODELS, PROGRAMS,
AND ISSUES

Deborah L. Floyd

This chapter has three purposes. First and foremost, it aims to identify and describe community college models for expanding access to the baccalaureate. Among these models are community colleges that confer these degrees and partner with others to provide the "net effect" of a baccalaureate degree experience for community college graduates. Much like the 1960s, this is an era of innovation: Community colleges are changing rapidly as an increasing number of them strive to "make good" on their promise of access by implementing diverse (and sometimes controversial) models of baccalaureate programming.

Second, this chapter seeks to encourage constructive dialogue on this topic, using pragmatic descriptors of current U.S. programming models. Third, it raises questions and issues that invite further exploration, especially in ways that will assist policy makers at the national, state, and local levels.

By way of fulfilling these three purposes, this chapter offers first a four-part typology of community colleges and baccalaureate degrees and then a look at how this emerging megatrend is shaping research, policy, and practice vis-à-vis community colleges.

To help illustrate these models consider the case of a fictitious student who embodies many of the characteristics of community college students that are relevant to the rationale for these baccalaureate models.

Martha Jane Smith is a 32-year-old first-generation college student enrolled in Rolling Hills Community College, a small rural college in the southeastern United States.[1] Her husband, Bill, is a union laborer who has worked construction all his life, like his father. They had the first of their three children when Martha Jane was only 16, and she dropped out of high school to take care of her family, as did her husband. Now, 16 years later, Martha Jane is taking time to pick up where she left off educationally, and she is a sophomore at the local community college.

Monday through Friday her three children ride the bus to rural public schools while she drops her husband off at his construction site and drives herself to classes at the community college, 22 miles away. When not in class, she spends most of her time in the college library using the computer and studying. Her goal is to earn an associate degree at the community college and eventually finish a bachelor's degree so that she can teach high school science and math classes in her hometown. "I want to be a teacher because I want to help kids learn," she said, "but I also know that a teaching job will bring me security and a good income." She is well on her way towards that goal and lacks only 15 semester hours to complete her associate of science degree.

Martha Jane is a determined woman who doesn't want to end up like her mother, who is completely dependent on her husband. So, three years ago, Martha Jane (who knew instinctively that an education would be a key to her independence) decided to earn her high school diploma by enrolling for GED classes at night in a local elementary school. Her oldest daughter babysat for the younger two children when her husband was busy with bowling or spent the evening "with the boys" at the union hall. As she continued her GED classes, Martha Jane's confidence in herself grew in tandem with her rising competence in math, science, communications, and other basic fields. In less than a year, she completed her GED and was on her way to fulfilling her dream of earning a college degree and becoming a high school teacher.

Thanks to advice and encouragement from her community college's GED professor, Martha Jane successfully maneuvered the bureaucracy

---

[1] This story is representative of many situations the author observed while serving as a president of a community college. Individual names, including people and the college, are fictitious.

of financial aid and received enough money to pay for her tuition and books. While she tested into a "pre college" English class, she enrolled for a full load of college-level general-education courses each term, and her grades have earned her a place on the college dean's list. Last semester she accepted an invitation to join the college's Phi Theta Kappa honor society, which has connected her with a network of new friends.

After completing courses next semester, Martha Jane Smith will be the first in her family to graduate from a college. But she knows that this associate degree is only one step towards the baccalaureate, another major hurdle before she will qualify to work in her chosen field. Private and public state universities have offered her scholarships, but she cannot accept those offers because the institutions are too far away from her home, and commuting would be prohibitively expensive and time-consuming. Rolling Hills Community College has several articulation agreements with area universities, and a few of them offer courses on its campus, but only occasionally and without consistency. For the first time in her college career, Martha Jane knows that the toughest step of her journey towards becoming a high school teacher lies ahead of her: How will she get access to the courses that she needs to complete a bachelor's degree?

Martha Jane, like so many place-bound community college students, is likely to become a victim of a system that promises access to a college degree but simply fails to deliver the necessary programs.[2] Fortunately, the GED program worked well for her as a seamless entry

---

[2] The Education Commission of the States (ECS) released a study, October 1, 2003, entitled "Getting Ready to Pay for College," part of a larger study by ECS to assist policy makers with efforts to increase attendance rates in higher education. According to ECS's president, Ted Sanders, "America is at risk for losing a vital ingredient for success—an educated populace" (Gomstyn, October 2, 2003 [online]). Sandra Rupert, director of the report and study, stated that the United States once was first in the world in baccalaureate-degree participation rates but now ranks eleventh because its rates did not grow while other nations invested in higher education and training (Mollison, 2003). The Lumina Foundation for Education has funded college-access projects, including one with the American Association of Community Colleges to address ways to increase access to the baccalaureate degree. While the United States once led the world in attainment of higher degrees, recent reports indicate that it is "losing ground."

to college. Like so many community college students, Martha Jane feels comfortable at the community college and would like to conclude her education locally, without having to leave her family and travel to a university. But unless the barriers that are now restricting her continued enrollment are removed, Martha Jane will be become a sad statistic, a would-be-teacher denied access to the necessary credentials for the teaching profession.

U.S. community colleges are noted for being responsive to community needs and addressing issues of access. They are "people's colleges" and the "last chance" for many individuals. These "open-door" institutions rarely turn away students as a demonstration of their commitment to access, at least until transition at the baccalaureate level becomes restrictive. States such as Florida led the way in mandating transfer of all community college credits and their counting towards state universities baccalaureate requirements. Most state universities and community colleges have articulation agreements that govern transfer into entire programs, but access may necessitate major and unexpected sacrifices. As some universities aspire to become more selective and research oriented, their emphasis on undergraduate education, especially off campus, often diminishes. Where does that leave Martha Jane, and many like her, who want to matriculate at a four-year college or university, but simply may not do so, given the transfer models currently available?

The topic of the community college baccalaureate has become extremely controversial, partly because of the lack of clarity in defining models and the use of an inconsistent, even confusing terminology. For example, the term "community college baccalaureate" has been used interchangeably to describe delivery models in which community colleges and universities collaboratively offer programs leading to the baccalaureate, with the university conferring the actual degree. Elsewhere, university branch and extension campuses conferring only associate degrees have recently added community college baccalaureates. Some community colleges that have added the baccalaureate to their degree offerings (without having a university partner) also use this term. Clearly, community colleges are trying to address increased need for access to the baccalaureate. Simultaneously, they are seeking a terminology to accurately represent a fundamental expansion in community colleges' mission.

Without question, community college educators would strongly agree that Martha Jane should have access to a bachelor's degree so that she might fulfill her dream. But, as the old adage goes, "The devil is in the details." Who will offer the upper-level courses? Who should confer the degrees? Where will courses be offered? Who will accredit these programs? And how will these programs be funded? Such devilish details complicate any well-intended desire to expand access to the baccalaureate for the place-bound.

A Four-Part Typology: Community Colleges and Baccalaureate Programs

Historical Context

Providing access to the baccalaureate was an early and central role of the two-year college. The first transfer agreement, adopted in 1903 by the University of Chicago and the new public junior college in Gary, Indiana, permitted Gary's young people to remain in their community for an additional two years before relocating to Chicago's south side (Pedersen, 2000).

The transfer function is a key role of community colleges with deep historical roots. Some commentators have argued that early junior colleges were established to permit universities to focus on upper-division instruction (Cohen & Brawer, 2003; Zwerling, 1976); others have asserted that they allowed place-bound students to remain at home for an additional one or two years of study before relocating to a university campus, law school, or medical college (Pedersen, 2000). Yet junior colleges never secured a monopoly over lower-division college instruction. Four-year colleges and universities never relinquished this role (Cohen & Brawer, 2003). Having retained a sense of control over the entire undergraduate curriculum, four-year colleges and universities became the "gatekeepers" of American higher education and used their power to approve (or deny) credits for "junior college" transfer courses.

Perhaps part of the underlying reason for the contemporary friction about the community college baccalaureate is that U.S. universities have had the authority to control the baccalaureate and this role has not been effectively challenged, until now. Those community colleges now proposing broad access to the baccalaureate may seem to threaten the power of universities to determine the baccalaureate curriculum and to award these degrees. While many argue that community college baccalaureate programs are "all about bumping up access for non-traditional students and helping to meet shortages like those in nursing and teaching fields," others fear that this movement could be counter-productive and mark the end of traditional community colleges (Troumpoucis, 2004, p. 6).

According to Cohen and Brawer (2003), "the community colleges have suffered less from goal displacement than have most other higher education institutions. They had less to displace; their goals were to serve the people with whatever the people wanted. Standing outside the tradition [of universities], they offered access" (p. 29). Today, community colleges are implementing numerous programmatic models and governance structures to deliver "whatever the people want." Increasingly, what people want includes proximate access to the baccalaureate, regardless of who confers the degree.

The typology offered here posits four models—articulation, the university center, university extension, and the community college baccalaureate—and reflects the author's best efforts to assimilate information from various sources. This list of institutions and models is not comprehensive, but is offered as a schema, with examples, to help shape the debate over the proper mission of community colleges. This typology may be useful to practitioners, researchers, and policy makers to study, compare, and contrast "like" programs. A comparison of key features that differentiate these models from one another is described in Table 3.1.

Articulation Model

Articulation agreements that ensure acceptance of freshman and sophomore credits by senior colleges and universities are vital to community colleges' transfer mission. In some states, such as Florida, associate degree graduates who complete a prescribed general-education core are guaranteed acceptance of credits and junior status at their state university. States such as California, Illinois, New York, Oklahoma, Tennessee, Texas, and Washington have transfer rates well above the norm because most of their community colleges participate in a collaborative project with a nearby four-year college or university, with procedures

Table 3.1 Comparison of Different Baccalaureate Models

	Articulation Model	University Center Model	University Extension Model	Community College Baccalaureate Model
Sequential attendance at community college followed by university	YES	YES	NO	NO
University uses community college facilities	NO	YES	NO	NO
Students complete baccalaureate degree at a campus other than the conventional university campus	NO	YES	YES	YES
University controls baccalaureate degree requirements	YES	YES	YES	NO
Community college controls baccalaureate degree requirements	NO	NO	NO	YES

governing student transfer spelled out in an intrastate agreement applicable to both institutions. In fact, according to a recent study of state policies and the success of community college transfer students, "effective state policies are at the heart of baccalaureate success for students transferring from two-year to four-year institutions with the goal of achieving their degrees" (Wellman, 2004 p. 1). Cohen and Brawer (2003) assert the articulation agreements become more effective when community colleges and universities collaboratively develop two-plus-two agreements in such specific program areas as teacher education, health, engineering, and agriculture and farm management.

With respect to teacher education, for example, recent studies report that almost 80 percent of U.S. community colleges (approximately 900 institutions) are implementing articulation agreements that encourage students to earn the first two years of a four-year degree at their local community college and also guarantee the full transfer of credits to a state university (Floyd & Walker, 2003; Hudson, 2000).

The dynamics of a community college student's transfer to a university, including the programmatic pathways and matriculation outcomes, have been the focus of numerous studies. Arthur M. Cohen (2003) describes the many roles that community colleges assume in assisting students with transfer transitions. He recognizes that there are models other than traditional transfer, which require community colleges' students to travel to an often-distant university for upper-division course work. New models, beyond the traditional two-plus-two models whereby students complete two years of study at the community college and transfer to a four-year college or university to finalize baccalaureate studies, are emerging. Some of these models include universities' offering upper-division courses on community college campuses. It is important to note that within the framework of the articulation model, creative three-plus-one models are becoming more popular (especially with propriety and private colleges) whereby students complete 90 hours with a community college and the four-year college provides the final year leading to a baccalaureate.

For many students, articulation models work well, but for others like Martha Jane Smith, a traditional articulation model is not feasible because she is unable to leave her family and travel to a university to continue her studies in a traditional on-campus format. While the

community college and university may have perfectly articulated transfer agreements, she is "place-bound" and needs relevant junior- and
senior-level courses offered locally.

University Center Model and Concurrent-Use Campuses

The university center model is becoming increasingly popular. Often
these centers are located close to or on community college campuses.
The university confers the degree in partnership with others, including
community colleges and sometimes other universities.

Implementation of this model often involves consortia of colleges
and universities that jointly use facilities for the delivery of upper-division
courses and programs. In Michigan, for instance, the Northwestern
Michigan College University Center includes 11 four-year universities
with programming that allows seamless entry to junior- and senior-
level course work from the community college. In Texas, North Harris
Montgomery Community College's university center includes six public universities that offer over 21 unduplicated bachelor's degree programs and 24 master's degree programs (Windham, Perkins, & Rogers,
2001). In south Florida, Broward Community College's central campus
is the home of the 4,500-student Florida Atlantic University campus
that is part of a much larger higher-education complex. The Edison
University Center, on Florida's Edison College[3] campus, is an alliance
among a number of regionally accredited colleges and universities that
houses several baccalaureate programs that articulate with Edison's
associate degree programs. Arizona Western College, located in isolated areas of Yuma and La Paz Counties, created a Yuma Educational Consortium with all levels of education providers, and they
also house buildings and programs provided by Northern Arizona
University.

Private and proprietary colleges and universities are becoming
increasingly active partners with community colleges in the delivery of
baccalaureate degrees on community college campuses, via distance learning and with university centers. For instance, through their bachelor

---

[3] Edison College was formerly Edison Community College. The College's name
was changed by the Florida legislature in late April 2004, House Bill 1867.

degree granting partner, Charter Oak State College (COSC) Bridge-point Education (formerly Charter Learning) accepts 90 hours of transfer credits and offers the final year of upper-division courses on community college campuses in Arizona and Washington State, with plans to expand to California and other states soon (Scott Turner e-mail communication April 27, 2004). COSC is accredited by the New England Association of Schools and Colleges and is a public college in the Connecticut state university system. Bridgepoint Education is a private for-profit organization founded in 1999, and has offered degree completion programs at corporate sites such as Boeing, BF Goodrich, and the National Guard. Their first community college agreement was with the Maricopa County Community College District colleges in 2001, and later with Arizona's Pima Community College and Washington's Skagit Valley College. Another example of the three-plus-one university center partnership is the relationship between Regis University and Colorado's community colleges through online and on-site delivery of courses. Regis University, accredited by the North Central Association (NCA), launched a new initiative called Associate's to Bachelor's ™ and in January 2004, hired Joe D. May, a former community college president, as its executive director of partnerships.

These are just a few of the many examples of the university center approach to delivery of the baccalaureate. These centers often engage private, proprietary, and state institutions as partners and may include online and on-site course delivery.

This model of joint-use facilities has emerged since the 1960s as a popular approach embraced by a number of states. According to the findings of a 1999 survey of State Higher Education Executive Officers (SHEEOs) on joint-use facilities (Windham, Perkins, & Rogers, 2001), 20 states reported the utilization of joint use facilities.[4] The governance models vary and include joint boards, local college governance, private boards, and some that are led by individual directors and presidents.

---

[4] States reporting joint-use facilities include Arizona, Colorado, Florida, Hawaii, Idaho, Illinois, Kentucky, Mississippi, Nebraska, New Jersey, Ohio, Oklahoma, Oregon, South Carolina, South Dakota, Tennessee, Texas, Utah, Virginia, and Wisconsin. The Windham, Perkins, and Rogers (2001) article in the *Community College Review* includes a more thorough analysis.

While the university center and concurrent-use models are not new, they are gaining in momentum and becoming increasingly popular. In Chapter 5, Albert L. Lorenzo describes various university centers and frames the discussion with a typology of six models: co-location, enterprise, virtual, integrated, sponsorship, and hybrid. The hybrid model is just that, a hybrid of other models, with one major addition—the community college is authorized to confer certain baccalaureate degrees.

Various forms of the university center model have been quite effective for expanding access to the baccalaureate and beyond to thousands of students. In fact, for Martha Jane Smith, the university center model may help her to obtain her baccalaureate in teaching. She would be dependent, however, on the university's keeping a promise to offer the courses (even if they had small enrollments) and to do so on a schedule that would allow her to complete her degree requirements locally.

University Extension Model

Universities have long provided baccalaureate education through off-campus and extension centers. Indeed, this was the mandate of the land-grant institutions from their inception. More recently, private and proprietary, as well as public institutions have seen this as a viable means of furthering their mission.

The twenty-first-century definition of the university extension model has various interpretations. Some colleges use their university affiliation in their own name, despite their own independent accreditation. Diverse forms of state governance further blur distinctions. Hawaii, for example, has given three of the University of Hawaii's community colleges (Honolulu, Kapi'olani, and Maui) approval to award the baccalaureate (Patton, 2003). West Virginia's Parkersburg Community College became the University of West Virginia in Parkersburg in 1989 and received legislative authority to grant the baccalaureate four years later. Westark Community College, Arkansas's oldest community college, became the University of Arkansas at Fort Smith in 2002 after a few years of offering four-year degrees. All the above institutions are associated with a university title, but they are independently accredited.

Another example of a university extension model for baccalaureate programming is the Louisiana State University—Alexandra, which was granted legislative authorization to move toward four-year status and by 2003, had reorganized itself. Its plans include officially completing the conversion by fall 2004, along with a tuition increase (www.lsua.edu/community/4year.htm). An interesting plan is the Pennsylvania State University plan that authorizes 14 of its 17 branch campuses to offer baccalaureate degrees to address unmet needs of place-bound students (University Colleges of Technology, 1997).

Oklahoma State University (OSU) is unique among land-grant institutions in possessing two independently accredited campuses that deliver certificate and associate degree education in technical areas. OSU's Okmulgee campus won state approval in 2004 to award baccalaureates in specialized areas that articulate with its associate degree programs.[5] This development seems to be congruent with the traditional focus of land-grant universities and the original federal mandate for "mechanical and practical arts."

The university extension model is similar to the university center model in that baccalaureate courses are offered at a campus other than the main or largest campus of a university, however, in the university extension model, the campus where these courses are offered is formally part of the university.

No doubt, these university extension programs have been very successful in expanding access to the baccalaureate, especially in workforce areas. In theory, for students like Martha Jane, these university extension programs could present seamless opportunities to earn the baccalaureate, if offered in a timely and accessible format in the areas that the student needs. In practice, however, programs such as teacher education are not commonly offered through the university extension model.

Community College Baccalaureate

The term "community college baccalaureate" describes various models of delivery, including those described in the models discussed previously. Most frequently, however, it denotes community colleges that

---

[5] OSU's Okmulgee technical campus proposal to offer specific baccalaureate programs was approved by the OSU Board late in 2003. The Oklahoma Board of Regents unanimously approved the plan February 13, 2004.

now "confer" the baccalaureate, not just partner with others for baccalaureate programming. A possible definitional problem associated with the term "community college baccalaureate" is that in some classification systems, a community college might be reclassified when it begins to offer baccalaureate degrees—even a single baccalaureate degree. For example, it appears that the practice of some, but not all, accreditation associations is to classify institutions according to the highest degree the institution awards. In such a case, a two-year institution that gains approval to offer a few baccalaureate programs would be reclassified as a four-year institution, even if the institution's intention is to remain effectively a community college, but one that offers a few baccalaureate programs. In reality, what we find in the field is the emergence of a new institutional type that embodies characteristics of different existing institutional types. The choice for classification is somewhere between trying to fit this new institutional type (imperfectly) into existing classification systems and developing a new way of classifying and describing these hybrid institutions.

An example of such a new way of classifying these hybrid institutions is the approach taken by The Southern Regional Education Board (SREB).[6] The SREB identifies those as associate/baccalaureate institutions, community colleges that grant mostly associate degrees but also some baccalaureates; specifically, Dalton State College and Macon State College in Georgia, and West Virginia University at Parkersburg.[7] It also includes University of Arkansas at Fort Smith (formerly Westark College) and will soon add Florida's community colleges that are (or will be) offering four-year degrees: Chipola, Miami Dade, St. Petersburg, and Okloosa Walton.

---

[6] SREB comprises Alabama, Arkansas, Delaware, Florida, Georgia, Kentucky, Louisiana, Maryland, Mississippi, North Carolina, Oklahoma, South Carolina, Tennessee, Texas, Virginia, and West Virginia.

[7] Dalton State College began offering the baccalaureate in 1998 in three types of management studies: industrial operations, information systems, and technology. Macon State College began offering these programs in 1997 in communications and information technology, health information, human services, health services administration, and BSN nursing. Parkersburg Community College (West Virginia University at Parkersburg) began offering these programs in 1993. The classifications listed are as of 2002.

Similarly, three community colleges in Texas (Brazosport College, Midland College, and South Texas Community College) were granted authorization by the Texas Coordinating Board to offer baccalaureates in certain applied technical and science fields in July 2003 (Larose, 2003; Wertheimer, 2003). In time, they will become SREB "hybrids," even though the Southern Association of Colleges and Schools (SACS), their regional accrediting association, will classify them as four-year institutions, not community colleges.

In 2001, a task force of the North Central Association's (NCA's) Higher Education Commission issued a report with recommendations for dealing with community colleges' requests to offer four-year programs.[8] The report explains the task force's deliberations; in each case, the NCA classifies community colleges offering and conferring four-year degrees as four-year colleges. In fact, according to NCA's executive director, Ron Baker, five colleges have "moved from associate institutions to baccalaureate institutions and received accreditation at the baccalaureate level while retaining accreditation at the associate level" (e-mail communication with Ron Baker, October 1, 2003).

In 1993, Utah Valley Community College's name and status changed to Utah Valley State College, as a part of its initial baccalaureate candidacy; in 1995, it received accreditation at the baccalaureate level in several areas. Similarly, Utah's Dixie College became Dixie State College of Utah in 2000, during the candidacy phase, and obtained final accreditation in 2002. NCA gave Montana's Salish Kootenai College candidacy in 1990 and accreditation for baccalaureate offerings as of 1993. NCA granted Great Basin College in Nevada candidacy in 1999, initial accreditation in 2003 with formal accreditation awarded retroactively to September 1, 2002 (Danny Gonzales, June 23, 2004 personal communications).

The University and Community College System of Nevada's elected Board of Trustees governs all state postsecondary institutions. Great

---

[8] The North Central Association (NCA) includes Arizona, Arkansas, Colorado, Illinois, Indiana, Iowa, Kansas, Michigan, Mississippi, Nebraska, New Mexico, North Dakota, Ohio, Oklahoma, West Virginia, Wisconsin, and Wyoming.

Basin College, in an isolated northern area, received approval in 2002 to confer baccalaureates in elementary education, integrated and professional studies, electronic instrumentation, and management technology; nursing is currently in development (Gonzales, 2003).

Thus a community college that is adding a baccalaureate emphasis, but keeping associate degree programs, may still fit the model of the community college baccalaureate. This "hybrid" institution is the result of a strong push to offer baccalaureate opportunities in communities.

For Martha Jane Smith, the other models—articulation, university center, and university extension—may not meet her needs, since partnerships with four-year colleges do not always result in appropriate courses being taught locally and in a timely manner. It is reasonable to assume that Martha Jane may not achieve her dream of being a high school teacher . . . at least not without a new model that offers relevant upper-division courses locally. If denied access to the baccalaureate, she would be justified in voicing her frustrations to leaders of the local community college (and anyone else who would listen) in hopes that it will take the lead by gaining approval to grant the baccalaureate. If the systems of four-year colleges that control the upper-division course work of the baccalaureate are unresponsive to this woman, who is typical of many place-bound students who deserve a chance to succeed in college, the local institution may have to do the "right thing" and lead the way toward implementing a community college baccalaureate.

A Mega-trend: Research, Policy, and Practice

Keeping current with local and state developments in community colleges and other associate degree–granting institutions that are petitioning for legislative and governance approval to confer baccalaureates is a challenge for even the most competent journalist. For instance, a bill introduced in California in early 2003 (Sturrock, 2003) would allow community colleges to offer upper-division courses jointly with the California State University System, although the model is unclear in terms of which institutions would confer the degrees. Also, in 2003, a failed South Carolina bill (Grimsley, 2003) would have allowed Trident

Technical College to add one bachelor's degree to its offerings—culinary arts.[9] In suburban Chicago, Harper College has been exploring four-year degree offerings (*Community College Times,* 2003; Granderson, 2003); an editorial cautioned local leaders to "go slowly on the four-year degree idea" and to look at states with four-year community colleges, such as Arkansas, Florida, Texas, and Utah (*Daily Herald Reports,* 2003). Unquestionably, news sources across the country will continue to cover these evolutionary changes in baccalaureate programming. But, in the absence of clear and consistent terms and concepts to describe these approaches, some reported information may not be accurate, at least to scholars studying technical details.

Recent Research

Surprisingly, there is little research published about the specifics of national and state policies and practices related to the community college baccalaureate. While models and partnerships abound, specific information consists of anecdotal news and stories, opinion-editorial articles, a few journal articles, and a handful of doctoral dissertations. Clearly, these new programming areas are ripe for publications and research. This section looks at two recent related documents.

Floyd and Walker Survey

As an ancillary focus, one recent study of state practices in teacher education programming may be of interest. In 2002–2003, Deborah L. Floyd and David A. Walker (2003) surveyed state directors of community colleges and asked if one or more colleges in their state were awarding bachelor's degrees in teacher education. Thirty-three responded to their

---

[9] According to a March 17, 2004 press release posted to the college's Web site (http://www.tridenttech.edu/ttcnews/3-17-04-bill-dh.html), legislation was passed by the 2004 South Carolina Legislature (after overriding the governor's veto). Prior to offering this degree, approvals must be gained from the South Carolina State Board for Technical and Comprehensive Education and the Commission on Higher Education. According to May 3, 2004 electronic mail communications from Kaye Koonce, general counsel for Trident Technical College, the College plans to submit the program proposal paperwork to the State Tech Board and the Council for Higher Education by mid-Summer, 2004.

survey, for a 64 percent response rate, which yielded a sample representative of U.S. community colleges. Only two states, Florida and Nevada, responded "yes" (community college baccalaureate model). Almost 20 percent responded "yes" but added that these degrees are being awarded through partnerships with universities (university center model). Further, almost 80 percent of U.S. community colleges are implementing articulation agreements for teacher education, suggesting the dominance of the articulation model. Community colleges in Florida and Nevada that may now confer the baccalaureate are four-year colleges to their regional accrediting associations, although clearly the state directors still view them as community colleges.

Community College Baccalaureate Survey

In mid-2003, the Community College Baccalaureate Association (CCBA) commissioned an independent study to ascertain interest among U.S. community college presidents in organizational and programmatic issues related to the delivery of baccalaureate programs, including the community college baccalaureate model.[10] Researchers sent surveys to 500 presidents selected randomly and received 101 responses, a response rate of slightly over 20 percent. Among the key findings, presidents would prefer to partner with a "mission complementary" four-year university in hopes of delivering baccalaureate degrees locally (CCBA, 2003).

Other major findings of this study of presidents are as follows:

- Many presidents indicated that their state legislatures have considered, or are planning to consider, expanding the baccalaureate through community colleges.

- Over half noted that community college-based baccalaureate programming is not completely understood by the state's higher-education community and policy makers.

---

[10] The contractor for this study was The Education Alliance from Framington, Massachusetts and the Community College Baccalaureate Association owns these unpublished data.

- Not surprisingly, interest in baccalaureates is greatest in areas where students are place-bound, such as isolated rural communities.

- Colleges that have expanded the baccalaureate through one or more of these models have done so in key academic areas such as business, computer science, criminal justice, education, elementary education, and nursing.

- Almost half of the colleges already offer some form of baccalaureate programming on their own or in partnership.

- Over a third of respondents indicated that four-year institutions in their area are not meeting baccalaureate demand.

- More than one-third affirmed that the majority of their students do not transfer to four-year colleges and universities because of geographical or financial barriers.

- Over two-thirds agreed that there are specific, high-demand career fields that require a baccalaureate and that currently the four-year institutions in their area are not meeting these demands.

- Approximately a fourth had received requests from area employers to offer the baccalaureate in certain fields.

- Over one-third affirmed that their faculty and staff have expressed interest in developing the capacity to offer baccalaureate programming on their campus.

- Approximately half noted that several of their academic programs are well positioned for transition to four-year offerings, including having the necessary faculty, infrastructure, and technology.

- Most have not completed a feasibility study or needs assessment or otherwise researched the impact of, or need for, a community college baccalaureate in their service area.

- Almost half affirmed personal interest in participating in a national association advocating community college-based baccalaureates.

Critics may argue that these findings represented the views of just slightly over 100 people and thus might not be representative of all U.S.

community colleges. However, this survey of presidents offers the most current research about this topic and is useful for practitioners and policy makers. Further, and more important, its findings offer much food for thought regarding the need to frame and address issues of policy, research, and practice.

Issues for Policy and Research

The ramifications of what appears to be a mega-trend among community colleges focusing on baccalaureate programming are many and multidimensional. The mere fact that current research is woefully inadequate to addressing these trends is troubling and offers an opportunity well worth embracing. One must wonder why national policy groups and associations have not been placing more emphasis on this trend. Is it because this topic is controversial so people imagine that not talking about it will make it "go away"? Perhaps associations, groups, and individuals have not fully grasped the enormity of this movement and the increasing pressures community college leaders face from students and communities to provide better opportunities for baccalaureate access. Or does the lack of engagement merely reflect normal inertia and uncertainty in the face of new challenges? Do some people look at community colleges' baccalaureate programming negatively and as involving "status creep" (Pedersen, 2001) or "mission creep" (Mills, 2003), or do they believe that colleges should "stick to what they do best" (Wattenbarger, 2002) and not take on baccalaureate programming?

Regardless of the reason, the time is overdue for state, national, and local policy makers, organizations, and leaders to recognize that this trend is very real and is begging for attention and focus. It necessitates articulation of a common language (terminology), such as the typology proposed in this chapter, to facilitate meaningful and useful policy studies and research. Foundations and other funding agencies should encourage the Community College Baccalaureate Association (CCBA) to serve as a convener to discuss relevant issues and as a documenter of this movement. The CCBA has been playing this role with very limited fiscal resources while dealing with an area of enormous interest to community college presidents and leaders.

Policy Issues

This mega-trend poses a number of other questions, such as:

- Is there truly a community college baccalaureate degree, since most regional accrediting associations view community colleges that confer the baccalaureate as four-year colleges?

- Do the regional accrediting associations, the Carnegie classification system, and organizations such as the SREB and AACC need a new scheme that recognizes these "new" colleges that are shifting to baccalaureate programming? What are the projected ramifications of such a move and of doing nothing in this regard?

- Is this movement actually a natural evolution of the community colleges' mission and promise of access to educational opportunities for the masses?

- If four-year colleges and universities do not respond to the underserved, who will, if not community colleges?

- What are the ethical and moral responsibilities of community colleges in terms of access to relevant baccalaureate programs after completion of the associate degree? Should they ensure that students understand fully the ramifications of a baccalaureate from each of the models proposed in this chapter, including the reality that some universities might not accept these baccalaureates as entry for graduate study and beyond?

- What are the specific curricular areas of emphasis and are they primarily workforce related or "new baccalaureates" rather than more traditional programs?

- As more universities are closing their doors to transfer students and cutting back for financial reasons, what will happen to community college students who need and want a baccalaureate but are not served by universities? Will community colleges seek new ways of providing access to baccalaureate programs without depending on universities?

- When universities shift focus and emphasize research while downplaying undergraduate education, should community colleges alter their missions and concentrate on the baccalaureate?

- How will these programs be funded? If community colleges are taking on baccalaureate programming, will universities relinquish state-appropriated monies for those functions and corresponding curricular control?

- What role do faculty members assume in these models of baccalaureate programming? What policies and practices will best sustain morale, fairness, support for their work, and other factors?

Research Issues

- One must ask who is responsible for this research agenda? Who will ensure that a timely, relevant research agenda is implemented for the benefit of practitioners, policy makers, researchers, and students? Will policy decisions rely solely on emotion and political factors, or will a research agenda help drive policy decisions? One hopes that this movement will catch the eye of influential leaders and organizations so that meaningful research can become part of this history in the making.

- There is a critical need for research about this mega-trend. But useful research requires a common language. The models of articulation and two-plus-two programming, university center, university extension, and community college baccalaureate must serve as discrete models. Not all baccalaureate programming that involves community colleges comprises a community college baccalaureate. There are many effective models whereby community colleges are providing access to the baccalaureate, in meaningful ways, without conferring the degree.

Conclusion: A Pressing Need

For Martha Jane Smith, and thousands like her in the United States, the issue of *who* confers the baccalaureate is not as important as having the accessible and affordable courses leading to that degree. Like the place-bound community college student who recently won the CCBA essay contest (McKinney, 2003), Martha Jane also wants access to the baccalaureate immediately after graduation from the community college.

Community college leaders are justified in their concern about providing access for graduates, such as Martha Jane, when better and more secure jobs require a baccalaureate. When times are toughest, universities and other four-year colleges are likely to close doors of opportunity to people like Martha Jane Smith, and community colleges will once again be struggling to keep the name of "people's college" by demonstrating their commitment to access in creative and new ways that make good on the promise of the "open door."

References

Cohen, A. M. (2003). *The community colleges and the path to the baccalaureate*. University of California–Berkley: Center for Studies of Higher Education. www.repositories/edlib/cshe/CSH4-03

Cohen, A. M., & Brawer, F. B. (2003). *The American community college* (4th ed.). San Francisco: Jossey Bass.

Community College Baccalaureate Association (CCBA). (2003). *Baccalaureate Needs Assessment Survey*. Unpublished survey results available from the CCBA offices at Edison College, Ft. Myers, FL.

Daily Herald Reports. Go slowly on four-year degree idea. *Daily Herald*. Retrieved September 8, 2003 from www.dailyherald.com/search/main_story.asp?intID= 37872128

Floyd, D. L., & Walker, D. A. (2003). Community college teacher education: A typology, challenging issues, and state views. *Community College Journal of Research and Practice, 27*(8), 643–663.

Gomstyn, A. (October 2, 2003). Nation faces a college-access crisis, education policy group warns. *Chronicle of Higher Education*. Retrieved October 2, 2003 from www.chronicle.com/prm/daily/2003/10

Gonzales, D. A. (2003). *Great Basin College*. Presentation delivered March 14–16, 2003, to the Community College Baccalaureate Association Conference, Phoenix, Arizona. Available from the author at dgon1@gwmail.gbcnv.

Granderson, K. (September 7, 2003). Four years at Harper? *Daily Herald*. Retrieved September 18, 2003, from www.dailyherald.com

Grimsley, J. A. (January 20, 2003). Letters to the editor: Culinary arts program. *Post and Courier*. Retrieved October 13, 2003, from www.charleston.net/stories/013003/let_30letters.shtml.

Hudson, M. (2000). *National study of community college career corridors for K–12 teacher recruitment*. Belmont, MA: Recruiting New Teachers, Inc.

Illinois College Considers Offering Baccalaureate. (September 29, 2003). *Community College Times, 16*(4), 10.

Larose, M. (July 8, 2003). Three Texas community colleges to offer bachelors. *Community College Times, 15*(15), 5.

McKinney, D. T. (April 14, 2003). We need a baccalaureate now. *Community College Week, 15*(18), 4.

Mills, K. (2003). Community college baccalaureates: Some critics decry the trends as "mission creep." *National CrossTalk.* Published by the National Center for Public Policy and Higher Education. www/highereducation.org/crosstalk/ct0103/news0103-community.html

Mollison, A. (October 2, 2003). Too few go to college, reports say. *Atlanta Journal Constitution.* Retrieved October 2, 2003, from www.ajc.com/paper/editions/Thursday/news_f3b71da411be913D00

Patton, M. (May 27, 2003). University of Hawaii reorganizes community colleges. *Community College Times, 15*(11), 10.

Pedersen, R. P. (2000). *The Early Public Junior College: 1900–1940.* Unpublished dissertation, Columbia University.

Pedersen. R. P. (July 23, 2001). You say you want an evolution? Read the fine print first. *Community College Week,* 4–5.

Sturrock, C. (February 10, 2003). Bill alters community college role. *Contra Costa Times.* www.bayarea.com/mld.cctimes/5146642.htm

Troumpoucis, P. (April 12, 2004). The best of both worlds? *Community College Week, 16*(16), 6–8.

University Colleges of Technology Alfred-Canton-Cobleskill-Delhi-Morrisville. (1997). *Report on the applied baccalaureate: A new option in higher education in the United States. May 1997.* Available from the United States ERIC Clearinghouse. Document number JC 970–340.

Walker, K. P. (2001). *An open door to the bachelor's degree.* www.league.org/publication/abstracts/leadership/labs 0401.html

Wattenbarger. J. (2002). Colleges should stick to what they do best. *Community College Week, 13*(18), 4–5.

Wellman, J. V. (2004). *Policy Alert.* Summary of *State Policy and Community College Baccalaureate Transfer.* San Jose, CA: The National Center of Public Policy and Higher Education. Available on line at www.highereducation.org

Wertheimer, L. K. (July 19, 2003). Three Texas community colleges to grant bachelor's degrees. *Dallas Morning News,* B1 & B5.

Windham, P., Perkins, G., & Rogers, J. (2001). Concurrent use: Part of the new definition of access. *Community College Review, 29*(3), 39–55.

Zwerling, L. S. (1976). *Second best: The crisis of the community college.* New York: McGraw Hill.

4

THE COMMUNITY COLLEGE BACCALAUREATE IN CANADA

ADDRESSING ACCESSIBILITY AND WORKFORCE NEEDS

Michael L. Skolnik

The community college baccalaureate movement in Canada dates back to the late 1980s.[1] By the year 2003, governments in three of Canada's four largest provinces had authorized community colleges to offer the baccalaureate degree. All told, more than a quarter of Canada's community colleges now offer at least one baccalaureate program, and that proportion will likely rise to almost two in five within the next year.

This chapter first describes Canada's community colleges to elucidate the context in which baccalaureate degrees have emerged. It next looks at the experiences of three provinces—British Columbia, Alberta, and Ontario—that permit colleges to grant bachelor's degrees. It then

[1] The author wishes to thank the following for input to this chapter: Paul Byrne, president and Janet Paterson-Weir, vice president (Academic), Grant MacEwan College, Edmonton, Alberta; Judy Eifert, vice-president (Academic), Mount Royal College, Calgary, Alberta; Brian Carr, dean, faculty of science, mathematics, and technology, Kwantlen University College, Surrey, British Columbia; and C. Neil Russell, vice president (Academic), University College of the Cariboo, Kamloops, British Columbia. The author's appreciation for the input that these individuals provided does not diminish his responsibility for the accuracy of the information in the chapter or for the opinions expressed.

examines the types of baccalaureates awarded by Canadian and U.S. community colleges and their impact on their institutions, offering a classification scheme to facilitate comparisons. It turns then to key issues raised by the degrees and next considers how they relate to potential reshaping of postsecondary education in Canada. The conclusion outlines their implications for policy, practice, and research.

Canada's Community Colleges: Provincial Creations

Canada is a federation, and its constitution—dating back to 1867 and revised substantially in 1982—spells out the division of powers between the federal government and the ten provinces. Education is under the jurisdiction of the provinces, which, since World War II, have jealously and zealously guarded that power. Between the early 1960s and the 1970s, provinces established non-university postsecondary institutions. Several called them community colleges,[2] but others deliberately avoided that term. For example, Ontario, after much deliberation, called them colleges of applied arts and technology (CAATs).

Unlike the United States, where generally the local authorities set up community colleges, in Canada it was the provinces that did so,[3] intending these institutions to meet certain social, economic, cultural, and political objectives. As college environments and provincial conditions varied across the country, so too did college systems.

John Dennison and Paul Gallagher (1995) identified five models in Canada. First, the most populated province (Ontario) and the least populated (Prince Edward Island) intended colleges to complement universities,

---

[2] In Canada, the word "college" when used without a modifier invariably refers to a community college. When Canadians wish to denote a four-year institution they use the term "university." Thus "going to college" means something quite different in Canada than it does in the United States. Following the Canadian practice, when I use the word college by itself in this chapter, I mean community college.

[3] Though the original decision to create community colleges in British Columbia was made by the provincial government, the means consisted of amendments to the Public Schools Act empowering local school boards to establish the colleges. Over the years, however, the college system in British Columbia became centralized though perhaps not as highly so as in other provinces.

serving mainly young people not eligible for university and preparing them for the workforce. In Ontario, colleges were to serve as an alternative to universities, and the two sectors were famously two solitudes into the 1990s, when serious attempts at coordination and articulation emerged (Skolnik, 1995).

Second, Alberta and British Columbia (BC) created comprehensive community colleges, modeled on California's that combined university transfer with technical-vocational programs. Whereas BC community colleges provided second-chance opportunities, in Alberta "most second-chance students were still directed to government-run vocational centres established throughout the province" (Dennison and Gallagher, 1995, p. 385).

Third, Manitoba, New Brunswick, Newfoundland, the Northwest Territories, and Yukon developed "the postsecondary vocational-technical college, without any transfer function and with a much stronger accent on shorter term work-entry training programs than on more advanced technological education" (p. 385). Newfoundland later incorporated transfer into the colleges' mandate. It was the lesser emphasis on more advanced technological education that originally differentiated these systems from Ontario's.

Fourth, Saskatchewan had both "colleges without walls" in rural areas and technical institutes in cities. The former operated as brokers, arranging for provision of educational services by other institutions and community agencies. This part of the model was "effectively set aside in the late 1980s when four previously independent technical institutes were reconstituted as a new multicampus Saskatchewan Institute of Applied Science and Technology and the more rural community colleges began to provide, as well as broker, educational services" (pp. 385–386).

Fifth, the most distinctive model was Quebec's, which based a system of colleges of general and vocational education (CEGEPs) on European experience. Situated after grade 11, these colleges had two streams—university preparation for two years (required for university admission in the province) and career preparation for three years. Adult education and short-term vocational training were not part of their original mandate, but, Dennison and Gallagher note, most soon became active in the former.

Given this variation among provinces, it is difficult to generalize about Canada's community colleges. In comparison to U.S. colleges, however, Canadian institutions give more prominence to vocational training. In Ontario, for example, they offer three-year career programs that are highly specialized and quite sophisticated.

Canadian colleges' strong emphasis on advanced career education has helped shape their baccalaureates in the three provinces where they are available—British Columbia, Alberta, and Ontario. Typically in Canada, two- or three-year programs result in a diploma. College spokespeople have long expressed concern that these diplomas are not internationally recognized and do not represent the level and content of the programs. Many college leaders believe that what these graduates have achieved is almost equivalent to a baccalaureate, though with different content than a typical university degree program.[4] Insofar as this perception is valid, the suggested solution is for colleges to lengthen career programs to four years and award baccalaureates somehow different in name from those offered by universities.

Because so many colleges concentrate on career education, it is difficult to say exactly how many *community* colleges there are in Canada. For example, are technical institutes and adult vocational education centers in fact community colleges? How about single-field institutions such as the Nova Scotia School of Fisheries and the Maritime Forest Ranger School? As a result, Statistics Canada, the national statistical reporting agency, for years avoided the term "community college" in favor of the umbrella phrase "Non-University Postsecondary Education Institution" for postsecondary institutions that do not award degrees. Now it reports data on "Community Colleges and Related Institutions." A 1999 government publication using data from Statistics Canada, listed 204 such institutions, but many of these are not typical community colleges—for example, the numerous radiation-therapy training facilities associated with hospitals (Education Indicators in Canada, 2002). The Association of Canadian Community Colleges lists

---

[4] The associate degree designation presently is limited mainly to British Columbia. As it is awarded after two years, it is considered to represent less than a three-year diploma.

154 member institutions on its Web site (ACCC, 2003). Not all CEGEPS are members of ACCC, but on the other hand, the ACCC list includes multiple campuses of some institutions. The best estimate of the number of community colleges in Canada would seem to be about 150.

There are 76 universities in Canada, and, thus at least twice as many community colleges. In contrast, comparable figures for the United States were 1,406 universities and 1,184 community colleges in 2000[5] (Carnegie Foundation, 2002).

The higher ratio of community colleges to universities in Canada than in the United States is associated with differences in the relative attainment of postsecondary credentials in the two nations. In the year 2000, the United States led Organization for Economic Cooperation and Development (OECD) countries with 28 percent of its working-age population having a baccalaureate or higher. Canada was fourth, with 20 percent (Education in Canada, 2003, p. 10). In proportion of population whose *highest* level of educational attainment is a college credential, Canada was second (to Ireland), with 21 percent, compared to 9 percent for the United States. However, there appears to be a trend toward closing this gap. A recent report shows that for persons aged 25–34 the proportion with a university degree is slightly higher in Ontario than in a group of peer American states (DesRosiers, 2003).

Although the education gap between the United States and Canada may be declining, it has persisted for a long time and has received much attention from economic policy makers in Canada. Analyses of economic policy in Canada often attempt to explain the Canadian—U.S. income gap partly in terms of different levels of education between the two countries. The earliest such study attributed about one-third of the 25 percent difference in per-capita income between the two countries in the early

---

[5] These figures exclude private, for-profit institutions, of which there were 15 universities and 485 associate's colleges in 2000. The Canadian figures given above exclude comparable non-university type institutions (there are no for-profit universities in Canada). I have also excluded the 46 combination baccalaureate-associate's colleges in the United States because of ambiguity about which sectoral category they should be included in, although as of 2000 they were mostly university-type institutions. Also excluded are specialized institutions like free-standing medical schools and tribal colleges and universities.

1960s to higher U.S. educational levels (Bertram, 1966). A recent study by Ontario's Institute for Competitiveness and Prosperity (2003) attributed 21 percent of the $7,000 difference in gross domestic product (GDP) per capita between urban Ontario and urban regions of a peer group of American states to higher educational levels in the latter.

Given that the Canadian—U.S. baccalaureate gap mirrors differences in relative numbers of universities and community colleges, one approach to the problem would be for Canada to increase spending on universities relative to community colleges, and the report just cited recommends doing that. An alternative route would be to enable community colleges to offer baccalaureate programs.

If one agrees that more baccalaureate degrees in Canada would raise per-capita income, how then to produce the greatest economic gain relative to the expenditure—expand the universities or have colleges deliver baccalaureate programs?

Community Colleges and the Baccalaureate Degree: Three Provinces' Experiences

Like many educational innovations in Canada, the movement for community college baccalaureates originated in the west; it started in British Columbia and Alberta and surfaced later in Ontario. In the late 1980s public concern surfaced over the fact that British Columbia had a relatively low completion rate for baccalaureate degrees, which some people thought was limiting its economic growth. A government-appointed Access Committee noted that British Columbia ranked ninth among provinces in degrees awarded and seventh in university participation rate. As well, access to degree programs was particularly difficult in remote regions (Dennison, 1997). At the time, most of the province was remote from a university—two universities were in the Vancouver area, and the other across the water in Victoria.[6]

---

[6] There was also an Open Learning Institute (later to be known as the Open Learning Agency) which included an open university, but which had not yet made much of an impact in providing baccalaureate degrees, and one small private denominational university in the province.

The Access Committee recommended that the more densely populated regions outside the Vancouver and Victoria areas institute complete baccalaureate degree programs by having their community colleges add the third and fourth years to the two years that they were already providing in selected program areas (Dennison, 1997). The province accordingly designated three of its sixteen community colleges to do so (Cariboo, Okanagan, and Malaspina) and soon added a fourth (Fraser Valley). Initially, one or more universities would award the degrees through partnerships with the colleges, but after a few years the colleges were able to grant the degrees themselves. In 1995, the authorities gave a fifth college (Kwantlen), which was near two universities, power to grant applied degrees, but not traditional degrees in arts and science; despite strong urging, they did not define "applied" (Carr, 2001). All five institutions changed their names to "university colleges" to reflect their new hybrid status.[7] In June 2003, all five were still members of the ACCC and, except for Kwantlen (still giving just applied degrees), all had been admitted to the national association of universities.[8]

By 1999, the university colleges were offering 82 baccalaureate programs—50 in arts and science and 32 applied or professional

---

[7] Until that time, in Canada, the term "university college" was used mainly to refer to a college affiliated with a university. It is still used that way in some other provinces, though not in British Columbia. A university college that is in some ways similar to those in British Columbia was established, in a different context, in Nova Scotia in 1974. University College Cape Breton was the result of merging a junior college campus of St. Francis Xavier University with Nova Scotia Eastern Institute of Technology. UCCB has a strong focus on economic development for Cape Breton Island and continues to offer both arts and science baccalaureate programs and community college-type programs in technology and trades (Christie, 1997).

[8] As this book was going to press, the restriction on the types of degrees that Kwantlen University College could offer was lifted and Kwantlen is now permitted to offer academic degree programs, the first being in psychology (Charlton and Hamilton, 2004). In another recent change of policy, all the community colleges in British Columbia, as distinct from the university colleges, will be permitted to offer applied degree programs. In yet another new development, the Government of British Columbia announced that one of the university colleges, Okanagan, was going to be replaced by a new University of British Columbia Okanagan and a new Okanagan College (Government of British Columbia, 2004). The postsecondary education scene in British Columbia is anything but dull!

(University Colleges Consortium, 2000). Many programs were regionally based—for example, the Bachelor of Science in Freshwater Science at Okanagan and the Bachelor of Arts in First Nations Studies at Malaspina.

Whereas the primary motivation for the BC reforms was to increase access to conventional university degree programs, neighboring Alberta enabled community colleges to offer baccalaureate programs to respond to the labor market. In 1995–96, the province introduced applied baccalaureate degrees for its community colleges and technical institutes as part of a six-year demonstration project to determine the value of this new type of credential. Initially the project consisted of only eight programs. A review committee concluded in 1998 that the experiment was a success and recommended continuation of the applied degrees; the government later announced that they would be a permanent feature (Government of Alberta, 2003a).

The applied degrees address the province's need for career preparation. They are four-year programs that combine six semesters of formal instruction with two of formally credited work experience. The Ministry of Advanced Education and Career Development reviews colleges' proposals for such programs. The proposals must show, among other things, evidence of labor-market demand over and above that for related diploma programs and employers' strong support for the work-experience components.

As of July 2003, the province had approved 27 applied-degree programs at nine of its sixteen public colleges and at both technical institutes. Programs covered resource-based fields such as applied petroleum engineering technology; human-service fields such as applied human-services administration; and high-technology areas such as applied information systems technology.

The Alberta colleges had two major functions: university transfer and career education. As Andrews, Holdaway, and Mowatt (1997) noted, Alberta acted before any other province in many aspects of postsecondary education—for example, concentrating all teacher education in the universities and establishing Canada's first community college (Lethbridge, in 1957), its first open university (Athabasca, in 1970), and its first comprehensive provincial mechanism to facilitate transfer (the Alberta Council on Admissions and Transfer, in 1974). Believing that its transfer programs were working well and that no additional universities were necessary, it introduced applied baccalaureate degrees in its public colleges—another first.

Ontario established community colleges primarily for career education and set up no systemic links with universities. Both sectors were content with this arrangement until the 1990s, when the colleges found barriers to their students' advancement increasingly problematic. In general, Ontario universities resisted overtures for effective transfer agreements, and the colleges had to develop such relationships with universities outside Ontario, principally in the United States; through distance arrangements with open universities in British Columbia and Alberta; and with a few enterprising universities in Australia. However, forcing students to look outside the province seemed an inadequate solution. Some college officials were openly critical of the universities' resistance; the universities were resentful of such criticism, and relations between the sectors became antagonistic. The colleges mounted a two-pronged attack—pressing the government to impose some kind of transfer policy and mechanism on the universities and campaigning for authority to award baccalaureate degrees themselves.

As it turned out, the political dynamics made the latter action more feasible than the former. In the mid-1990s, under a new and neoconservative government, the universities' monopoly over degree granting had become an issue. Ontario had a long history—under different political parties—of hostility towards the idea of private universities, but the new government favored privatization in areas heretofore regarded as public monopolies (such as health care and electricity). It also appeared to believe that postsecondary education should primarily foster economic growth. However, except for replacing a small portion of the universities' general operating grants with targeted funding to serve its innovation agenda, it showed the traditional deference towards university autonomy in academic matters, including admission of transfer students.

The cabinet was preparing a major piece of legislation to open up degree granting to other providers, including private, corporate, and proprietary ones, and now piggy-backed on it a provision to allow community colleges to offer applied baccalaureate programs that could be shown to meet the needs of the labor market. This provision addressed both the colleges' desire for their students to have greater access to the baccalaureate and the need voiced in several reviews of postsecondary education for more polytechnical programs (Skolnik, 1989; Smith, 1989; Pitman, 1993). For example, a former chair of the Science Council of Canada had promoted high-level technical education that combined academic and applied study (Smith, 1989). The universities did not like the idea of the colleges being able to award any degrees, but in public hearings on the legislation they concentrated their attacks against private universities entering Ontario, which they saw as a greater threat to their monopoly.

The legislature passed the Post-Secondary Education Choice and Excellence Act in December 2000. Applications from colleges to offer applied degree programs go for review to the Postsecondary Education Quality Assessment Board (PEQAB), which also reviews applications from other types of institutions seeking to offer degree programs.[9] As in Alberta, the initiative started as a pilot project—in this case, with a provision that the minister could approve up to 24 applied-degree programs. However, before the pilot period ended, the minister approved more than 24, and it looked as if applied degrees had become a permanent feature. As of June 2003, the minister had allowed 18 colleges to offer 39 such programs. Examples are Bachelor of Applied Information Sciences (information security systems), Bachelor of Applied Technology (photonics), and Bachelor of Applied Arts (human-services management).

The PEQAB has produced the most detailed standards for such programs in Canada, and perhaps anywhere.[10] Programs must comprise eight semesters of on-campus study and at least one separate, paid, full-time co-op work term of at least 14 consecutive weeks. At least

---

[9] The author is a member of this board, having been appointed to it by the Minister when the board was established. He has also been intimately involved in some of the prior events described in this section of the chapter, having been commissioned by a joint body of the two sectors to write a discussion paper on college–university relations (Skolnik, 1999) and having chaired a historic meeting between officials of the two sectors that produced an accord on transfer between sectors (the Port Hope Accord).

[10] The Handbook and other documentation regarding the degree programs are available on the Board's Web site (http://www.peqab.edu.gov.on.ca).

20 percent of the courses must be outside the main field of study. The college's application process includes a site visit and report by an assessment panel normally consisting entirely or mostly of university professors. While skepticism, if not hostility, toward the new degrees is fairly common among university administrators, almost all assessments have been quite positive.

Classifying and Comparing Baccalaureate Initiatives in Canada and the United States

Figure 4.1 classifies community colleges' recent baccalaureate initiatives in Canada and compares them with the United States. The columns distinguish intentions for the degree (more access to traditional degree versus a new type of degree), and the rows, intentions vis-à-vis the institution (adding a new function versus creating a new type of institution); of course, actual outcomes may differ from original intentions.

The distinctions in the figure refer to predominant tendencies, and some overlap is likely. For example, while the community college might hope to offer the same type of degree typically offered by universities, its distinctive environment may make the student's experience quite different. How much is a degree a function of curriculum, and how much of the environment of study? The offering of baccalaureates now in two very different types of institutions may enable researchers to gain some insight into this question.

One of the first areas of development of baccalaureate programs in the United States has been teacher education, a field where programs are commonly offered by universities. Canada has concentrated on having community colleges offer a new, more applied type of degree to meet workforce needs in fields where programs are not commonly offered by universities. This is the exclusive focus of community college baccalaureate programs in Alberta and Ontario (see box 2 of Figure 4.1).[11] Of course, there are some U.S. examples of the latter—for instance,

---

[11] An early report of the newly approved community college baccalaureate in Texas suggests that with its apparent applied orientation toward and connection to the needs of local industry, it may have a lot in common with the Alberta and Ontario degrees (Wertheimer, 2003).

	Intended nature of baccalaureate	
Intended effect on institution	Expanding access to conventional university degree	Introducing a new type of degree
Adding an additional function	**1** Examples in the United States are teacher education and nursing programs; none in Canada Examples: Great Basin College (Utah) St. Petersburg College (Florida)	**2** The predominant type in Canada; some in the United States Examples: Colleges in Alberta and Ontario Westark College (Arkansas)
Creating a new type of institution	**3** Only Canadian examples: Four university colleges of British Columbia (Cariboo, Fraser Valley, Malaspina, and Okanagan) Dixie State College (Utah)	**4** Examples in Canada: Kwantlen College (British Columbia) (prior to 2004) Institutes of technology and advanced learning (ITALs) (Ontario) University of Ontario Institute of Technology

Figure 4.1   Canadian and U.S. Community Colleges and Baccalaureate Initiatives

Arkansas's Westark College (see box 2) (Tanehill and Connor, 2001)[12] and perhaps New York's colleges of technology (Call et al., 1997), and there has been an increasing emphasis on this type of program in the United States. The only Canadian example of using community colleges to expand access to conventional degrees is the BC conversion of four community colleges into university colleges (see box 3; Kwantlen appears in box 4). As noted earlier, the concept of an applied degree has been elusive, and several forces may cause applied degrees to become more like conventional academic degrees—for example, the influence of accreditation, the stature of the university, and the professional socialization paths of faculty members.

Intentions pertaining to institutional mission are usually pretty clear when colleges receive permission to offer baccalaureate degrees. For example, in authorizing public colleges to offer such programs in selected fields, Alberta made it very clear that the colleges' fundamental mission was to remain the same:

> Public colleges and technical institutes offering applied degree programs will not become universities, nor will they confer degrees in traditional university programs. . . . The intention of the applied degree demonstration project is to allow public colleges and technical institutes greater flexibility to fulfill their traditional mandate which is providing career and technical education and training to Albertans at the certificate and diploma level. (Government of Alberta, 2003b, p. 2)

In contrast, the BC government intended transformation of some community colleges into university-colleges (see box 3) "to create a new type of institution that offered the best of both university and college programs and services to the region" (University Colleges Consortium, 2000, p. 3).

---

[12] The distinction between "conventional" university type and new applied degree programs is not an easy one to make. Great Basin College's first baccalaureate program was a B.A. in Elementary Education (Gonzalez, 2000) which seems like a degree that universities have long been offering. However, Chapter 9 describes the efforts of the college to make this program quite different from elementary education programs typically offered at universities.

In regard to institutional change, an American college such as St. Petersburg (see box 1) stands somewhere between the Alberta and BC cases, but probably closer to Alberta. Although the name changed from St. Petersburg Junior College to St. Petersburg College, the legislation states that: "St. Petersburg College shall maintain the policies of a Florida community college, including the open-door admissions policy and the authority to offer all programs consistent with a public community college's authority" (Florida Legislature, 2001). The new statute seems to add a substantial new function while retaining the core of the college's previous mission. In contrast, when Dixie College became Dixie State College, its president stated, "We are not a community college offering B.S. degrees. Dixie State College of Utah is an accredited four year institution" (Huddleston, 2000, p. 3).

If St. Petersburg suggests the need for finer gradations than those in Figure 4.1, recent developments in Ontario (see box 4) make that need even clearer. In February 2003, the provincial government designated 3 of its 24 community colleges as Institutes of Technology and Advanced Learning (ITALs) and another the Institute of University Partnerships and Advanced Studies (Ontario Ministry of Training, Colleges and Universities, 2003). The ITALs may have up to 15 percent of their programs in applied baccalaureate degrees, as opposed to a limit of 5 percent in other colleges. They are expected also to have greater involvement in applied research and more emphasis on industry support for new programs. Although these four newly titled institutions remain colleges of applied arts and technology (CAATs), they seem to portend a new type of institution, though not as different from their former counterparts as the BC university colleges are from theirs.

In a related development, the province authorized one of the new colleges to start up a technical university under a common governing board. The University of Ontario Institute of Technology (see box 4) has a quite different mandate from other universities. It is to meet employers' needs in its region and facilitate transfer between community college and university programs. Although its charter suggests a hybrid of community colleges and universities, various forces may push it in the direction of the other universities—for example, accreditation, local desire for a university like those in other communities, and academic norms.

Three Key Issues

In the short life of the community college baccalaureate in Canada a number of issues have arisen. However, as there are few data available, official documents and impressions that I obtained in talking with college administrators and faculty members are my only sources for some tentative observations. Differences in the conditions for colleges to award baccalaureate degrees in British Columbia, Alberta, and Ontario make it impossible to generalize across the country. While a change in something as fundamental as credentials awarded could affect almost every facet of an institution's life, I limit this section to three central issues—access to graduate schools, effects on faculty members, and effects on colleges' future roles.

A common issue in discussions is access to graduate school. To date, eligibility of baccalaureate graduates to master's programs seems to vary among provinces. BC university colleges developed their first baccalaureate programs in collaboration with universities, which initially offered the degrees. Thus, these degrees enabled admission to graduate study at those universities, which appears to have continued even after the university colleges began awarding degrees themselves. The status of the later, applied baccalaureates is less clear. Normally, however the university college and the university communicate about the development of these programs, which may provide the opportunity for exploration of possible pathways to graduate study. In professional fields such as business and nursing, it seems quite possible for graduates to go on to master's programs.

Although Alberta's colleges attempt to keep in touch with their graduates and have tried to help at least a few baccalaureates apply to master's programs, I could not locate any study of the experience of such graduates. The impression I was given is that graduates with applied degrees normally needed additional undergraduate studies to qualify for graduate school. The government Web site states that "students wishing to pursue graduate studies after an applied degree may be required to take additional course work since four years of academic study are generally required as a prerequisite for entry into graduate programs."

As noted earlier, Alberta's applied degrees involve three years of academic study and one year of paid work experience. However, there are still many three-year baccalaureate programs in Canadian universities, and graduates from many of them may enter some master's programs.

Three years of classroom study, however, may not allow for the amount of general education that universities require for admission to graduate school. The Alberta government's requirement of a year of paid work experience reflects its original intention to prepare candidates for employment, in effect making the degree a terminal academic credential. However, as the colleges seek to develop lifelong learners, which could include graduate school, the colleges' and the government's views seem to conflict.[13] I was told about two graduates of applied baccalaureate programs in Alberta who were admitted to MBA programs at Canadian universities, one in Manitoba and the other in Ontario. Further, one Alberta college now has an agreement with a university-level institution in Nova Scotia under which graduates of certain of the college's applied degree programs will be admitted to the MBA program in Nova Scotia. Apparently, community colleges in Canada are following the same circuitous routes to help graduates of their applied baccalaureate programs get into graduate school as many have had to follow to help their transfer students move on to a suitable program in a university.

The first graduating classes in Ontario are still a few years away. The PEQAB intends its standards to make the degrees "real," and so admission to graduate school afterwards may well be possible. In contrast to Alberta's degrees, Ontario's involve eight semesters of classroom study and have breadth requirements. However, experience suggests that graduate schools outside Ontario will recognize the new qualifications well before Ontario universities do so.

---

[13] This aspect of the debate about the applied baccalaureate degree gives a sense of déjà vu to those who recall a similar debate about the applied associate degree. At one time it was widely assumed that the associate degree in applied areas was a terminal educational credential. Indeed, Brint and Karabel's (1989) widely discussed criticism of community colleges, that they limited the educational opportunity of their students, was based on equating "vocational" with "terminal." However, as Arthur Cohen noted, more students transfer to universities from vocational than from so-called transfer programs (Cohen, 1990).

A second major area of interest concerns the effects of the new initiatives on faculty members at community colleges, particularly in regard to hiring, tenure and promotion, work profiles and workload, academic freedom, and instructors' role in governance. The only empirical study of these matters that I am aware of is Laden's study of perceptions of college personnel in Ontario (Chapter 10). The BC reforms seemed to augur most for change in faculty role and working conditions, and from the beginning, many observers wondered how long it would be before the faculty's primary focus shifted from teaching to research. Yet, Carr reported that as of 2001, support for research was still quite limited (Carr, 2001). Recently, however, Canadian community colleges' access to research funding from national sources has improved significantly; one new competitive program, the Canada Foundation for Innovation Research Grants, awarded 27 colleges research funding, giving seven of them more than a million dollars each. These amounts are small compared to what the foundation gave to universities, but they suggest that college research is on the increase. Eligibility does not depend on colleges' offering baccalaureates, but there does seem to be a synergy between baccalaureate degrees and research funding. Further, the university colleges in BC have received some of the new Canada Research Chairs. Nevertheless, the university colleges are still under the same legislation as community colleges with respect to collective bargaining and determination of faculty work conditions, and this may well inhibit emergence of more university-like work profiles there.

Given how much more restricted the Ontario initiative is than the BC one in regard to both the nature of the degree and the change in institutional mission, one might expect a smaller impact on faculty in Ontario. Still, in my frequent interactions with members of the Ontario college community, I hear again and again expressions of concern (or, among a few, hope) that the colleges' new baccalaureate degrees will make the Ph.D. and research mandatory for instructors.

Potential changes in faculty roles relate to a third, larger concern about whether degree-granting colleges will maintain their commitment to their traditional mission. Provincial governments have made very clear their expectations that the baccalaureate will augment rather than replace other functions, and college presidents who have initiated baccalaureate programs commonly indicate their agreement with this position.

Nevertheless, the baccalaureate may unleash forces that will reshape the college in the image of the university.

The Baccalaureate and Postsecondary Education in Canada

In addition to looking at it as an innovation in its own right, we should consider the community college baccalaureate within the overall structure of postsecondary education, which has been responding to a variety of challenges, including globalization, advances in information technology, and the demands of the knowledge society. New providers of degree-level higher education have entered the once nearly exclusive preserve of public and private not-for-profit universities. They include corporate universities; proprietary universities; media, publishing, and software companies; educational brokers; virtual universities; international consortia of universities; and other educational sectors that have not previously offered baccalaureate and higher degree programs (Cunningham et al., 2000; Middlehurst, 2002). Conventional universities have found the new suppliers so threatening that Britain's association of public universities has established a monitoring agency (Universities UK and the Higher Education Funding Council for England, 2000). Within this constellation of new providers, the community college may be the most credible in regard to dedication to academic quality and serving student and community needs.

One of the most difficult structural issues for education policy makers in Canada has been institutional differentiation (Jones, 1996; Skolnik, 1986). The Canadian university sector is relatively homogeneous, consisting of a disproportionate number of research universities for the size of the country and few specialized institutions, particularly technical universities. As I noted earlier, college sectors vary considerably across the country, but several provinces, such as Ontario, have little institutional differentiation among colleges.

In British Columbia, and more recently in Ontario, the community college baccalaureate has been part of an attempt to create greater institutional differentiation within postsecondary education, particularly in the non-university realm. As such efforts confer different status on particular institutions, they evoke jealousy among counterparts and pressure to extend the new status to the others, even though doing that would conflict with the goal of increasing institutional differentiation.

In both Alberta and Ontario, the new degrees may provide the type of higher-level technical education that Canada perhaps needs. Indeed, these two provinces have sought thereby to meet the needs of industry rather than expanding access to traditional degrees. In a major change in Canadian higher education, while community colleges have started awarding applied degrees, the country's few technical universities have disappeared,[14] in effect passing the responsibility for high-level technical education that combines academic with hands-on learning to the community colleges.

Will these community colleges continue to fulfill their mission of the last quarter-century, or in turn bequeath parts of that mission to other public institutions, such as adult vocational centers and community agencies? This would further alter the shape of postsecondary and adult education in Canada. In any event, it will be interesting to see over the next several years not only how the community college baccalaureate fares, but how it is positioned in a larger realignment of postsecondary education in Canada, and perhaps globally.

Issues for Policy and Research

Policy Issues

* Together, British Columbia, Alberta, and Ontario provide a rich body of models, experience, and, in some cases, documentation, which in total constitutes a valuable resource for any jurisdiction that is considering the introduction of a community college baccalaureate.

---

[14] Nova Scotia Technical University was closed in 1997, its programs being moved to Dalhousie University. The Technical University of British Columbia, which was established only in 1997, was closed in 2002, and its campus was taken over by Simon Fraser University. The former Ryerson Polytechnical Institute became Ryerson Polytechnic University in 1993, and perhaps confirming the widespread perception that it was becoming a mainstream rather than a technical university, changed its name to Ryerson University in 2002. The University of Ontario Institute of Technology is now Canada's lone technical university, and given the experiences of the others, it is not hard to imagine that it will come under pressure to become more like a conventional university.

- Some jurisdictions may find the BC university college a useful model for providing access to academic baccalaureate programs in regions that lack a university and for creating a hybrid community college–university.

- Probably no jurisdictions in North America have gone as far as Alberta and Ontario in developing and implementing, on a system-wide basis, the workforce baccalaureate catering to industry. Ontario's PEQAB has produced detailed curriculum and program standards for these programs that are available on its web site (Ontario Postsecondary Education Quality Assessment Board, no date). The site contains all the college proposals for such programs, some as lengthy as 200 pages.

- The concept of an applied degree that is equivalent in rigor to an academic degree but different in content has proven difficult to define in practice. The PEQAB in Ontario has explicated standards for the applied degree and described how it differs from an academic degree; for details, please see its handbooks. Differences between the two types of degrees may affect qualifications required of faculty members, curriculum models, and criteria for accreditation.

- How to balance state or provincial control over the degrees with institutional autonomy? The three Canadian provinces discussed all substantially involve government departments or agencies in the process, but each goes about approval and regulation differently.

Research Issues

- It seems that increasingly, postsecondary institutions are having to expand their missions to include ever more functions and activities. The three provinces examined in this chapter asked community colleges to add a major new function while maintaining their existing functions.

  – How well have these colleges stuck to their traditional goals while adding the baccalaureate?

- Could research into this experience shed light on the more general issue of multiple missions for community colleges?

- As the Alberta experience demonstrates, there may be a conflict between preparing applied graduates for employment and fitting them for postgraduate studies. This issue has affected professional and applied programs in universities, and thus the literature on professional education may be of use here.

  - Specifically, is conflict inevitable between preparing students in applied or professional programs for the workforce and preparing them for further education?

  - Are there other curriculum models for applied baccalaureate programs that would reduce or alleviate this conflict?

- The simultaneous existence of baccalaureate degree programs in the universities and in the community colleges, sometimes in the same or related subject fields, introduces possibilities for research related to the following questions:

  - Are there significant differences in the way that students experience an academic degree program in a community college compared to a university, even if the curriculum and credentials of faculty are roughly the same? Are there associated differences in student learning and retention between similar programs at the two types of institutions?

  - Related to the point made in the introduction about there being two ways to increase baccalaureate enrolment in Canadian postsecondary education, what are the benefits relative to the costs of increasing the number of baccalaureate degrees by expanding universities compared to having community colleges offer baccalaureate programs?

- The college baccalaureate, particularly the applied, or workforce, version of it, seems in large part a response to the challenges of globalization and the knowledge society. These challenges are transforming postsecondary education in a variety of ways, for example, in the growth of virtual education, corporate and proprietary colleges, and university partnerships with industry. If, rather than viewing the new qualification as an isolated phenomenon, we look at it in the context of postsecondary education in flux, certain questions arise:

- To what extent will being able to offer the baccalaureate help to maintain the competitiveness of community colleges vis-à-vis corporate and proprietary technical colleges?

- How strong is demand by employers for applied graduates in technical fields, and what are the longer-term career prospects for such graduates?

- How do the contributions of applied baccalaureate programs to the local and national economy compare to those of traditional academic baccalaureate programs?

References

Andrews, M., Holdaway, E., & Mowatt, G. (1997). Postsecondary Education in Alberta since 1945. In G. A. Jones (Ed.), *Higher education in Canada: Different systems, different perspectives* (pp. 59–94). New York: Garland Publishing, Inc.

Association of Canadian Community Colleges. (2003). *ACCC member list.* www.accc.ca/english/college membership_list.cfm

Bertram, G. W. (1966). *The contribution of education to economic growth.* Ottawa: Economic Council of Canada. Staff Study No. 12.

Brint, S., & Karabel, J. (1989). *The diverted dream: Community colleges and the promise of educational opportunity in America, 1900–1985.* New York: Oxford University Press.

Carnegie Foundation for the Advancement of Teaching. (2002). *The classification of institutions of higher education, 2000 edition.* http://www. carnegiefoundation.org/Classification/CIHE2000

Carr, B. (2001, Winter). The University College System in British Columbia, Canada. *CCBA Beacon, 2*(1), 2–7.

Charlton, S. & Hamilton, K. (2004). *The first two years of a new undergraduate psychology degree: Problems and solutions.* Presented at It's About Access: Fourth Annual Conference of the Community College Baccalaureate Association, San Francisco, CA, February 28–March 1.

Christie, B. D. (1997). Higher education in Nova Scotia: Where past is more than prologue. In G. A. Jones (Ed.), *Higher education in Canada: Different systems, different perspectives* (pp. 221–243). New York: Garland Publishing, Inc.

Cohen, A. (1990). Review of *The diverted dream. Higher Education, 20*(2), 223–225.

Cunningham, S., Ryan, Y., Stedman, L., Tapsall, S., Bagdon, K., Flew, T. & Coaldrake, P. (2000). *The business of borderless education*. Canberra, ACT: Department of Education, Training, and Youth Affairs.

Dennison, J. D. (1997). Higher education in British Columbia, 1945–1995: Opportunity and diversity. In G. A. Jones (Ed.), *Higher education in Canada: Different systems, different perspectives* (pp. 31–58). New York: Garland Publishing, Inc.

Dennison, J. D., & Gallagher, P. (1995). Canada's community college systems: A study of diversity. *Community College Journal of Research and Practice, 19*(5), 381–394.

DesRosiers, E. (December 9, 2003). *A comparative analysis of the balance between college and university enrollment in the United States and Ontario*. Toronto: Association of Colleges of Applied Arts and Technology of Ontario. http://www.acaato.on.ca

Education in Canada: Raising the standard. (March, 2003). Ottawa: Statistics Canada. 2001 Census, analysis series.

Education indicators in Canada: Report of the pan-Canadian education indicators program, 1999. (2002). Ottawa: Statistics Canada and Council of Ministers of Education Canada.

Florida Legislature. (2001). SB 1162-2nd Engrossed, Signed by Governor Jeb Bush, June 6, 2001, Section 40, St. Petersburg College.

Gonzalez, D. A. (Fall, 2000). The Great Basin college experience. *CCBA Beacon, 1*(3), 4–5.

Government of Alberta. (2003a). *The Applied Degree—History*. http://www.learning.gov.ab.ca/college/AppliedDegree/history.asp

Government of Alberta. (2003b). *The Applied Degree—Frequently Asked Questions*. http://www.learning.gov.ab.ca/college/AppliedDegree/faq.asp

Government of British Columbia. (March 17, 2004). *News release: New UBC Okanagan to help add 5,500 student spaces*. Victoria: Office of the Premier.

Huddleston, R. (2000, Fall). The birth of Dixie State College of Utah. *CCBA Beacon, 1*(3), 2–3.

Institute for Competitiveness and Prosperity. (June, 2003). *Missing opportunities: Ontario's urban prosperity gap. Working paper no. 3*. Toronto.

Jones, G. A. (1996). Diversity within a decentralized higher education system: The case of Canada. In V. L. Meek, L. Goedegebuure, O. Kivinen, and R. Rinne (Eds.), *The mockers and the mocked: Comparative perspectives on differentiation, convergence, and diversity in higher education* (pp. 79–93). Oxford: Pergamon/IAU Press.

Middlehurst, R. (2002). *The developing world of borderless higher education: Markets, providers, quality assurance, and qualifications*. A paper presented at the First Global Forum on International Quality Assurance, Accreditation and the Recognition of Qualifications in Higher Education, UNESCO, Paris, October 17–18, 2002.

Ontario Ministry of Training, Colleges, and Universities. (February 10, 2003). *Backgrounder: Institutes of technology and advanced learning.* Toronto.

Ontario Postsecondary Education Quality Assessment Board (PEQAB). (n.d.). *Handbook for applicants: Applied degree programs, Ontario colleges of applied arts and technology.* www.peqab.edu.gov.on.ca

Pitman, W. (Chair). (1993). *No dead ends.* Report of the Task Force on Advanced Training to the Minister of Education and Training. Toronto: Ministry of Education and Training.

Skolnik, M. L. (1986). Diversity in higher education: The Canadian case. *Higher Education in Europe, 11*(2), 19–32.

Skolnik, M. L. (1989). *How Ontario's college system might respond to pressures for the provision of more advanced training.* A Report Prepared for the Ontario Council of Regents Vision 2000 Review of the Role and Mandate of the CAATs. Toronto: Ontario Council of Regents for the Colleges of Applied Arts and Technology.

Skolnik, M. L. (1995). The evolution of relations between community colleges and universities in Ontario. *The Community College Journal of Research and Practice, 19*(5), 437–452.

Skolnik, M. L. (1999). *CAATs, universities, and degrees: Towards some options for enhancing the connection between CAATs and degrees.* A discussion paper prepared for the Ontario College-University Consortium Council. Toronto.

Smith, S. L. (1989). *Skilled and educated: A solution to Ontario's urgent need for more polytechnic programs.* A Report Prepared for the Ontario Council of Regents Vision 2000 Review of the Role and Mandate of the CAATs. Toronto: Ontario Council of Regents for the Colleges of Applied Arts and Technology.

Tanehill, D., & Connor, S. (Winter, 2001). The manufacturing technology baccalaureate degree at Westark College. *CCBA Beacon, 2*(1), 1–2.

University Colleges of British Columbia Consortium. (February, 2000). *An exploration of issues facing the University Colleges of British Columbia.*

Universities UK (formerly Committee of Vice-Chancellors and Principals) and the Higher Education Funding Council for England. (2000). *The business of borderless education: UK perspectives.* London.

University Colleges of Technology: Alfred, Canton, Cobleskill, Delhi, and Morrisville. (1997). *The applied baccalaureate: A new option in higher education in the United States.* Albany, NY: State University of New York, Office of the Chancellor. Permission granted by R. W. Call.

Wertheimer, Linda K. (July 19, 2003). Three Texas community colleges to get bachelor's degrees. *Dallas Morning News.* www.dallasnews.com

5

THE UNIVERSITY CENTER

A COLLABORATIVE APPROACH
TO BACCALAUREATE DEGREES

Albert L. Lorenzo

It is often the simplest things in life that offer the greatest insight. Consider the children's game Crack-the-Whip. Its premise is simple: several skaters begin to join hands and then complete a series of sharp turns until the player at the end is finally set free. Each new person joining the line enables those who follow to skate faster, and the distance traveled by the one set free is the direct result of the momentum created by everyone who came before. Crack-the-Whip is an apt metaphor for the aspirations that each generation harbors for the next. It depicts a desire that transcends nationalities, income levels, and political beliefs. Parents want a better life for their children, and that hope invariably includes higher levels of formal education. For more than a century in the United States, community colleges have helped to make those dreams come true.

History has shown that educational attainment levels usually improve as national economies become more affluent. Greater wealth can provide more opportunities for learning, and expanding economies require better-educated citizens and workers. Each cycle builds a higher foundation for the next. Fortunately, the U.S. educational system has been able to respond to these ever-increasing demands, but it has often required bold new visions and innovative concepts. The evolution of community colleges is a prime example.

Looking to revitalize the country following its wartime sacrifices, President Harry Truman established the President's Commission on

Higher Education (Truman Commission) in July 1946. The purpose outlined by the president was very broad: "We should now reexamine our system of higher education in terms of its objectives, methods, and facilities; and in the light of the social role it has to play" (Truman, 1946). In 1946, only 11 percent of white Americans and 3 percent of African Americans aged 20 and over had completed a full year of college (Quigley and Bailey, 2003). Believing that postsecondary education would become increasingly important to the democracy and the economy, the commission recommended, among other things, creation of a network of public "community colleges" that, because of their convenient locations, would broadly extend learning opportunities from the twelfth to the fourteenth grade. "The time has come," it declared in its report, "to make education through the fourteenth grade available in the same way that high school education is now available" (President's Commission on Higher Education, 1947).

Now, just a few years into the twenty-first century, educational and public policy leaders are once again examining the social and economic benefits of higher education. Some are suggesting that the United States, to keep pace in the knowledge age, should raise its educational goal once again, this time to the baccalaureate level. True to their nature, community colleges are already developing innovative ways to provide greater access to four-year degrees, some by seeking new degree-granting authority, and others by employing a variety of collaborative methods and models.

This book presents a critical examination of the ways in which community colleges are enhancing access to baccalaureates. This chapter explores one proven route—a collaborative arrangement between two- and four-year institutions known broadly as the "university center." It begins by assessing implications of growing demand for baccalaureate education, describing how university center models build on a history of collaboration that enhances capacity and effectiveness, and suggests some benefits of university centers that go beyond access. It next describes six models differentiated by structure, location, programming, and the extent of the community college's influence. It then identifies strategies, benefits, and criteria for success that researchers and practitioners find in collaborative arrangements. The chapter concludes with public policy implications and opportunities for further research.

Growing Demand

Is there really a need for U.S. community colleges to develop university centers or to become otherwise involved in baccalaureate programming? Current trends in educational attainment and recent surveys of student aspirations suggest that the answer is "yes."

The increase in educational attainment among U.S. adults during the last half of the twentieth century is nothing short of spectacular. Many parents who wanted a better life for their children have not been disappointed. As Table 5.1 indicates, those 50 years saw continuous improvement in every category of educational attainment, including a remarkable four-fold increase in the proportion of baccalaureate degree holders. Many studies project that these trends will continue. If so, it will place even greater demands on already overburdened colleges and universities.

A national survey of high school seniors conducted in 1997 revealed that 77 percent would probably or definitely complete a four-year degree—up from 55 percent in the early 1980s (U.S. Department of Education, 2000). Other surveys find that most Americans believe

Table 5.1   Highest Educational Attainment Level (%) of Americans 25 Years of Age and Older

Year	Less Than High School	High School Graduate	Some College	4-Year Degree and Higher
1950	65.7	20.7	7.3	6.2
1960	59.0	24.6	8.8	7.7
1970	44.8	34.0	10.2	11.0
1980	31.4	36.8	14.9	17.0
1990	22.4	38.4	17.9	21.3
2000	16.0	33.1	25.4	25.6

Source: Derived from data reported by the U.S. Census Bureau available from http://factfinder.census.gov/servelet/DatasetMainPageServelet?

that attending college is a necessity to keep pace in the workforce (Overview, n.d.), and wage studies show that baccalaureates enjoy an increasing earnings advantage over high school graduates (Fitzgerald, 2000). As a result, many career-oriented students are now looking to continue learning, and a higher proportion of students who complete vocational degrees at community colleges have been transferring to universities (Cohen and Brawer, 2002). Even regional accrediting agencies considering how to assess the community college baccalaureate conclude that the four-year degree is becoming fundamental to career access and career mobility (Higher Learning Commission, 2000).

So the appropriateness (some might say the necessity) of community colleges becoming more active in baccalaureate education is finding justification in mounting concern that existing four-year institutions cannot meet future demand. Virginia's State Council for Higher Education, for example, recently concluded that by 2010, in the absence of significant expansion, its public four-year campuses would be turning away more than 6,000 students per year (Argetsinger, 2003). If we estimate conservatively that the increase in the proportion of four-year graduates over the next 20 years will only equal that of the last two decades, by 2020, more than a third of all adults living in this country will have sought to achieve at least a baccalaureate degree. University centers provide a practical and cost-effective means for meeting this increased demand.

Collaboration has helped higher education achieve many important goals, and the university center concept is a logical extension of this tradition. Neal (1988) points to extensive collaboration during the "golden years" of the 1960s and early 1970s, as institutions looked for a quick and reliable means to boost capacity. Collaboration was again common during the economic downturn of the 1980s and aimed at cost-effectiveness, consolidation, and, in some cases, self-preservation (Pritzen, 1988). Later, it became a suggested means to increase transfer rates for community college students (Cejda, 1999).

A comprehensive 1994 study of two-year–four-year collaboration (Smith, Opp, Armstrong, Stewart, & Isaacson, 1999) found that partnerships included a huge number of initiatives with a sweeping range of purposes. The 617 community college presidents responding to a national survey reported involvement in 9,990 partnerships at six geographical areas.

Among the purposes that they rated most important were articulation agreements (94.4 percent of respondents), two-plus-two programs (81.5 percent), and distance education (66.6 percent).

Today's university center collaborations incorporate many of these historic purposes, and as a result they have become a popular model for community colleges wanting to increase local access to baccalaureate degrees. Prather and Carlson (1994) were among the earliest commentators to study these partnerships and found that, while they varied in complexity, they emerged most frequently in response to excessive commuting distances, dominant transfer patterns, or when states restricted the number of four-year institutions. Their study was also one of the first to point out that, while university centers were similar in their overall goals, they took several forms.

Six Models

While the concept dates back to the 1960s, the phrase "university center" did not become common until the late 1980s. Today it is a generic term for several fundamentally different models where community colleges collaborate with one or more senior institutions to provide more convenient access to baccalaureate degrees. Almost all the models involve joint use of teaching and office space, most commonly situated on the two-year college campus.

A survey conducted by the Florida Postsecondary Education Planning Commission found that the most successful joint-use sites were at the local and regional levels, developed through collaborative partnerships that focused on workforce needs (Windham, Perkins, and Rogers, 2001). That survey also found that 85 percent of the responding facilities were the product of state governing boards, interinstitutional agreements, or both, but only three of the twenty states provided separate annual appropriations for joint-use programs. These joint-use facilities frequently served a unique segment of the population, usually working professionals, who might not otherwise be able to enroll in upper-division coursework.

Previous works have classified university center models by facility, location, number of partners, governance, programming, and delivery system (Cook, 2000; Kent, 2002; Prather & Carlson, 1994). This chapter proposes a new taxonomy, focusing on the role of the community college; its involvement with governance, financing, and operations; and its influence over academic programming. Six distinct models are proposed— co-location, enterprise, virtual, integrated, sponsorship, and hybrid—and where possible mention prominent or pioneering institutions associated with each model.

The Co-Location Model

As the name implies, this category includes instances where two- and four-year institutions deliver programming in the same physical location, most often on the community college campus. The upper-division coursework may be housed in a few classrooms, in a shared or exclusive-use building, or in what may be perceived as a branch of the senior institution. Although there needs to be a good working relationship between the institutions, the academic programs operate independently, and, where the community college owns the facilities, the interaction resembles that between landlord and tenant. The partnership rarely has dedicated full-time personnel, governance and decision-making processes are fairly independent, and each providing institution develops, evaluates, and refines the curriculum.

One pioneering example was an off-campus center of the University of Houston, which opened in a freestanding building on the campus of Victoria College (Texas) in 1973. The University of Houston Victoria Center, a response to local-workforce and related educational needs, offered only upper-division coursework. Proceeds from locally approved bond issues allowed Victoria College to fund the startup facilities. Still located on the community college campus, the center in 1983 became the University of Houston—Victoria, with permanent degree-granting status (About University of Houston—Victoria, n.d.).

The Enterprise Model

Under this model, several institutions form a consortium to develop and operate a higher-education center, usually in an underserved part of the state. Whether the facilities belong to a nonprofit corporation formed by the partners or to a member of the consortium, they usually have a collaborative governance structure. The community college becomes a joint-venture partner, typically with a proportional voice in operations, finance, and programming. The staffing and budget of each participating institution are usually proportional to its programming at the center.

Texas has evolved this model quite effectively in its multi-institutional teaching centers (MITCs). The Universities Center at Dallas (UCD), founded in 1994, was the first MITC, housed in a former downtown department store. The city of Dallas, the local business community, and the Alliance for Higher Education partnered to establish the UCD and have provided financial support (About Us, n.d.). Six state universities and the Dallas County Community College District offer undergraduate and graduate coursework at the center.

The University Center at Greenville (South Carolina) evolved from a mid-1960s "handshake" arrangement between the presidents of Greenville Technical College and of Clemson University (J. Drake, personal communication, July 24, 2003). Two decades later, Clemson invited other state-supported institutions to form a consortium, and the South Carolina Commission on Higher Education approved the Greenville Higher Education Center in 1987. Classes began two years later in a renovated factory adjacent to Greenville Technical, and the venture became known as the University Center of Greenville. In January 2001, the center, which now includes seven senior institutions and the community college, moved into 123,000 square feet of space in a renovated shopping mall owned by the Greenville Technical College Foundation. Clemson serves as fiscal agent for the consortium, and funds come from membership fees, a state appropriation, and a credit-hour charge paid by the institutions delivering courses at the center (Our History, n.d.).

Other noteworthy examples include the University Center of Rochester (Minnesota), the Auraria Higher Education Center (Colorado), and the University Center of Lake County (Illinois)—a nonprofit organization, whose 17 member colleges and universities will occupy a new 86,000 square-foot facility on the Grayslake campus of the College of Lake County in 2004.

The Virtual Model

This model is similar to many campus-based university centers, except that it offers upper-division coursework online rather than on-site. Still, the community college serves as a full partner and remains actively involved with upper-division students through to their baccalaureate graduation.

Without question, the Community College Alliance, developed by Franklin University in Columbus, Ohio, is the nation's premier example of the virtual model. The Alliance was the vision of Franklin's long-serving president, formerly a vice president at Macomb Community College in Michigan. He pilot-tested the idea with his former two-year institution in 1998, and by early 2003 more than 180 U.S. and Canadian community colleges had signed on. Students from 38 community colleges in 11 states completed the requirements for their bachelor's degrees through the program during the spring 2003 term (Record number of CCA students graduate, n.d.).

By design, Franklin's virtual approach makes many of the benefits of a university center program available to almost any community college. One of the few potential drawbacks is that students must learn online. The Alliance offers two types of contractual agreements to participating two-year colleges, depending on state regulations. The *partnership model* allows enrollees to continue using the student and academic support services of their community college through to graduation. The *articulation model* lets students take up to 24 hours of "bridge" coursework beyond the associate degree at their community college before completing the bachelor's degree online through Franklin (Community College Alliance, 2002). Both types of agreement authorize the partnering community college to confer the baccalaureate during their regular commencement ceremonies. Franklin shares a portion of the tuition fees with the community colleges to reimburse them for continuing services to Franklin students.

The Integrated Model

This model takes co-location to a higher level of coordination and collaboration. In fact, some of the more prominent examples evolved from a co-location center. Over time, the two- and four-year programs and related student services merge into the totality of campus life. Here the community college helps plan and identify programming needs and dedicates staff members to oversee use of space, course offerings, and technical support. Integrated university centers generally offer a broad range of baccalaureate and graduate-degree options, either through an exclusive arrangement with a single senior institution or by collaborating with several university partners. The facilities used may range from a few dedicated classrooms, to shared buildings, to freestanding complexes equipped with the latest technology.

Florida has developed several integrated university centers. Many involve a partnership between a community college and a single state-supported university. They make extensive use of two-plus-two programs, which build on a statewide articulation agreement that assures acceptance of associate-degree graduates at state universities. Brevard Community College and the University of Central Florida began their partnership under a co-location model in 1983, but over the years theirs has become one of the most integrated programs in the state. They not only share instructional facilities, but they now jointly manage a library, cooperatively hire faculty members and support staff, share sophisticated technology, and dually operate a one-stop student services center (J. Drake, personal communication, July 24, 2003).

Several community colleges in Michigan have developed integrated university centers by partnering with senior institutions. Alpena and Mott community colleges provide dedicated space in existing buildings, and Muskegon Community College's Center for Higher Education operates in a 93,500 square-foot freestanding building on its main campus. Community college students can transfer as many as 90 credit hours in certain well-articulated programs. Although Michigan does not provide operating funds to its university centers, it has given some community colleges capital outlay grants towards construction.

The Sponsorship Model

Under this model, the community college clearly leads in developing and operating the university center and determining its academic offerings. The two-year college recruits partners, obtains funding, owns and operates typically freestanding facilities, strongly influences academic programming, assists in evaluation, and retains a full-time staff dedicated to oversight and advancement of the center. Sponsored university centers generally engage several partners, both public and private, and offer a comprehensive array of upper-division and graduate programs in day, evening, and weekend formats.

Macomb Community College in Michigan probably pioneered the sponsorship model with its Macomb University Center. Initially funded in 1988 by a voter-approved tax levy that supports both capital and operating needs, the center opened its first freestanding building in 1991. It completed an Engineering and Technology Building in 1999. By the spring 2003 semester, it enrolled nearly 3,000 students in over 40 upper-division and graduate programs provided by nine partners. It also contains a Center for Executive and Professional Development.

Sponsored university centers are the most assertive means for community colleges to enhance access to upper-division coursework, short of obtaining authorization to grant baccalaureates. When properly designed and administered, they provide high-quality programs and services that satisfy students' expectations for a true collegiate experience. For example, Macomb routinely surveys its university center students and asks how their experience there compares with universities that they have attended in the previous five years. An impressive 85 percent of respondents over a five-year period rated it as "much better" or "somewhat better," while 97 percent would recommend it to other people.

The University Center at North Harris Montgomery Community College District in Texas and the University Partnership at Lorain County Community College in Ohio represent two other sponsorships. Both offer extensive programming in dedicated facilities through several university partnerships.

The Hybrid Model

A new "hybrid" model is emerging, which combines university center programming with authority to grant a baccalaureate. Georgian College in Ontario has been piloting university partnership programs for several years. Recently, it gained provincial ministry approval to become Ontario's first Institute of University Partnerships and Advanced Studies (an integrated model) and to offer its first applied degree, a Bachelor of Applied Business in Automotive Management, beginning in the fall of 2003 (B. Gordon, personal communication, August 8, 2003). A similar situation now exists at St. Petersburg College in Florida. That school has now received approval to offer three bachelor's degrees on its own, but it will continue to operate its University Partnership Center. Such a new hybrid approach has the potential to deliver the best of both worlds—collaborative degrees through a university center and baccalaureates through the community college.

Strategies and Benefits

Curriculum, Financing, and Staffing

As part of a broader research and planning initiative, a team from Macomb Community College reviewed the Web sites of nearly fifty U.S. and Canadian community colleges with university centers and later conducted in-depth telephone interviews with administrators from 15 centers operating under the integrated or sponsorship model (Champagne and Barrett, 2003). As one might expect, differing state and local requirements force variations in approach, but some commonalities surfaced.

University centers do not grant degrees. Rather, the partnering institutions award degrees, typically without noting on the diploma that the coursework took place at a university center. Specific program requirements and curriculum approvals reside with the providing institutions, and a growing number of four-year partners are accepting more than 62 credit hours, the typical credit requirement for an associate's degree, from the community college as transfer credit. Some partnerships, such as the Franklin Community College Alliance, encourage students to complete hours beyond the associate degree at the community college.

University center programs generally involve only non-lab-based curriculum, except for Macomb's mechanical, electrical, and computer engineering majors offered in partnership with Oakland University. Undergraduate and graduate majors in business, computer science, information technology, and education appear most frequently in university centers.

Programs for healthcare professionals are also popular, with the Bachelor of Science in Nursing (BSN) being quite common. Many of the larger institutions offer selected liberal arts majors, usually in English and the social sciences. Other popular degree majors include criminal justice, public administration, and certain applied technologies.

All of the university center administrators interviewed said that their institutions had formal articulation agreements linking them with university center degree programs. Some programs permit students to have dual enrollment and/or to take classes from several partner institutions. A few indicated that partners were developing joint degree options among themselves, thereby reducing the number of duplicate courses offered at the center.

The partnering institutions usually handle advice for upper-division students, with the larger programs having full-time advisors on-site. Community colleges often assist with information on general transfer and associate degrees. Brevard Community College's partnership with the University of Central Florida has a highly integrated student support component, using shared staff in a one-stop service center and joint staffing and operation of a library.

Because of widely varying state and local funding mechanisms, there are fewer commonalities in financing of university centers. The Florida study revealed that most states do not provide direct operating appropriations. In most cases, participants pay "rent" for classroom and office space on a per-credit-hour or selected pro rata basis. Northwestern Michigan College's foundation provides partial funding to its university center. Lorain Community College in Ohio charges a percentage of the tuition and state aid received by the partners.

Sources of startup or capital funding also vary widely. Some states, such as Florida and California, have provided startup money but then restricted the community college's ability to charge for facilities. Michigan and Ohio have made direct grants for capital outlay to help construct and equip a few university center facilities but without limiting the ability to charge rent. Direct ministry grants funded facilities at Georgian College in Ontario but not programming. Greenville Technical College in South Carolina developed facilities with significant philanthropic support. Other less common financing methods have included property tax levies and direct assistance from business and civic organizations.

In general, university centers operating under the integrated and sponsorship models have full-time staff members funded by the community colleges. The other models typically have community college staffers to coordinate programming, but are not fully assigned to the partnership. With one of the larger university center programs in the country, North Harris Montgomery County Community College District (Texas) employs 10 full-time staff members, including a director and advisors. Its 16-member University Center Council oversees program approvals and operations.

Finally, community colleges assist with marketing and recruitment activities at most university centers. At a minimum, they provide program information on their Web sites and links to further information from the partner institutions. Assessment, however, occurs less frequently. Fewer than half of the administrators interviewed reported formal program evaluations or student-satisfaction surveys.

Benefits beyond Access

An old saying imparts that the more things change, the more they stay the same. This holds true in higher education. For example, while the Truman Commission looked for ways to enhance access to higher education, it raised several other issues that still have relevance today.

The commissioners worried about the rising cost of a college education and that it was becoming a barrier for many people who could otherwise benefit. College tuition had risen 30 percent between 1939 and 1947 (Quigley and Bailey, 2003). Their report cautioned, "By allowing the opportunity for higher education to depend so largely on the individual's economic status, we are not only denying to millions of young people the chance in life to which they are entitled, we are also depriving the nation of a vast amount of potential leadership" (President's Commission on Higher Education, 1947). The repetitive double-digit tuition increases at many universities in recent years make the concern even more compelling today. But by improving ways for students to blend community college and university coursework, to continue living at home and working in the community, and to commute shorter distances, university centers make four-year degrees more affordable as well as more accessible.

Minority participation in higher education was also a concern of the Truman Commission. Then, like today, minorities lagged behind in both college-participation and degree-completion rates. Community colleges have historically served a greater proportion of minority students than universities, and they have developed considerable expertise in assisting special-needs and at-risk populations. If greater numbers of minority students could continue their baccalaureate studies on a community college campus, they could continue to avail themselves of these support services. Despite the lack of research on the subject, the probability of minority students' completing four-year degrees would probably increase through greater use of university center models.

Finally, the Truman Commission was anxious about the economy. The country was undergoing a transformation, shifting from wartime to peacetime production. It demanded new workers, veterans needed new skills, and reunited families had a strong desire to stay close to home. Community colleges seemed to be the answer, and they continue to offer local solutions to many of today's economic and workforce challenges. However, they can provide responses only through the associate-degree level. University centers allow them to move to a higher level of service, with corresponding benefits to workers, employers, communities, and the nation as a whole.

Community colleges are ideal for baccalaureate education through collaboration with four-year institutions. By capitalizing on their historic flexibility and responsiveness, university centers can go well beyond more traditional university extension centers by providing a "college experience" as well as a "college education" (Lorenzo, 1989). They can pay special attention to nontraditional students and help minority and at-risk individuals complete four-year programs. They can help develop the local economy and workforce and significantly reduce costs for students and their families. They are more cost-effective for state governments than expanding university systems. They respect institutional autonomy and curriculum processes, thus avoiding accreditation issues. Finally, they can link upper-division university coursework with the academically nurturing environment of a community college campus. When properly designed and implemented, university centers can provide benefits well beyond simply enhancing access to four-year degrees.

Strategies for Success

For all its promise, collaboration in higher education does pose risks. As a result, community colleges thinking about university center partnerships should look carefully at some well-researched and proven strategies that can assist them.

In one widely cited study, Patterson (1974) concluded that traditional belief in institutional autonomy forms a principal impediment to effective college-university cooperation. Neal (1988) strongly agreed, noting that cooperative arrangements seem to give colleges the best of both worlds: stronger academic programs with no loss of autonomy. Patterson proposed several principles to guide cooperative arrangements. They included improving the quality and range of education available to students, minimizing duplication of programming and redundancy of facilities, having a fundraising capacity for collective needs, and showing a mutual willingness to respond to changing needs and new clientele.

A well-articulated mission statement also helps. Jadallah's (1994) analysis of ways for school-university collaboration to increase educational opportunities found that clear communication of principles and ideals was essential to any collaboration. A clear mission statement promotes understanding of purpose and can increase alignment of outcomes from independent decisions.

Knoell (1990) found that voluntary agreements usually work better than those mandated by legislation or regulation. Her national study on transfer, articulation, and collaboration led her to believe that incentives for both two- and four-year institutions seem more effective than threats of punitive actions. Statewide agreements about policies and practices that arise from local or regional cooperation are more likely to be effectively implemented than those that lack grass-roots support.

A comprehensive study of community college consortia (Smith et al., 1999) asked presidents of two-year institutions to identify "very" or "somewhat" important elements for partnerships. More than 80 percent of respondents cited shared objectives, partners' capability, benefits for all, and cost-effectiveness. Other frequently mentioned factors were adequate staffing, partners' reputation, and formal contractual agreements.

The study also urged geographically proximate partners, to benefit the college's local service area.

Maintaining strong, positive relationships also contributes to program success. Based on years of private-sector research, Kanter (1994) notes that business alliances are living systems, evolving progressively in their possibilities. Relationships between organizations begin, grow, develop, or fail in ways similar to personal relations, and successful partnerships manage the relationship, not just the deal.

The opinions of practitioners closely parallel these research findings. Many of the university center administrators interviewed in the Macomb survey emphasized clear mission statements and strong relationships. They valued stable, yet flexible interactions; commitment to a common purpose; and listening to and respecting the unique needs of the senior institutions. Programs needed to be relevant, and those that directly responded to well-defined local educational needs typically attracted many students. Community colleges should do careful research, especially into educational needs in the local workforce, before launching new programs.

Reasons for Success

A casual search of the Internet will show many more university centers in the United States and Canada than community colleges that grant four-year degrees. This ratio is not likely to change dramatically soon. First, university centers offer ease of entry. Baccalaureate authority requires formal state approval, while most two-year–four-year collaborative arrangements do not. In many states, a university center can begin the day an agreement is signed, and it can do so in existing space on a community college campus. Neither institution needs to recruit new types of faculty, develop new curriculum, or approve new degrees. Perhaps more important, new accreditation is unnecessary. The baccalaureate granted by the partnering institutions already has accreditation, and usually respect, in the community and the marketplace.

Current politics and economics also seem to favor university centers. The movement for community college baccalaureates has sparked considerable opposition from universities and even from some two-year colleges, and at least one state board is encouraging more four-year programming on two-year college campuses (Haynes, 2001). Other critics argue that community colleges do not have the financial resources to offer programs that are as academically rigorous as those at traditional four-year institutions (Brophy, 2000). There is some concern that allowing them to grant advanced degrees will necessitate additional state funds for upper-division instruction. Already hit by shrinking state resources, many four-year institutions may use their political clout to oppose creation of more baccalaureate-granting institutions.

There are also some contradictions within the movement. While there is a strong case that community colleges should gain the right to confer a type of "applied" baccalaureate typically not provided by senior institutions, much of the authority granted so far covers more traditional university programs and majors—as in the education degrees recently authorized for two community colleges in Florida. This practice raises questions of mission and duplication.

Some opponents have argued that such authority will gradually undermine the community college's traditional mission more than would creating university centers. There is some reason to believe that this is true.

Community colleges receiving baccalaureate authority in both Arkansas and Utah eventually became state colleges, and within months of receiving such authority two Florida community colleges chose to drop the word "community" from their names. The *Chronicle of Higher Education* has reported that, although officials at Miami-Dade College say that it will always be a community college, it is slowly beginning to behave like a four-year institution. The institution already wants to add more bachelor's degrees and expand its honors college, and it is launching a $250 million fund-raising campaign (Evelyn, 2003). Only time will tell who is right.

One thing does seem certain, however. Aspirations for baccalaureate education will continue to grow, and, true to their heritage, community colleges will search for ways to respond. Whether by gaining degree-granting authority or by collaborating in university centers, they seem destined to play an expanding role in helping students achieve baccalaureate degrees.

Issues for Policy and Research

Policy Implications

The continuing growth and development of the various university center models should cause educational and political leaders to consider a number of important public policy needs, including:

- Realistically forecasting the capacity of state universities and assessing their ability to accommodate the expected increase in student demand for baccalaureate degree programs;

- Determining to what extent the growing popularity of online learning modifies the anticipated need for expanding physical access to baccalaureate degrees;

- Deciding whether the cost-effectiveness of university center programs should inspire separate state appropriations and alternative funding models to support construction and operation of these centers;

- Exploring alternatives to mandated data-reporting systems that will allow for research on the efficiency and effectiveness of university centers, especially as they compare to other methods for increasing access to four-year degrees;

- Identifying a means for state and federal financial aid programs to recognize and accommodate the special academic circumstances of dually enrolled and university center students; and

- Discussing how to provide greater incentives for two-year–four-year collaboration in addressing a broader range of emerging student and societal needs for higher education.

Future Research

Because university centers are relatively new, research efforts have provided only descriptive narratives and occasional status studies conducted by organizations considering the development of new centers. There are very few reliable data available to support traditional research, and current reporting systems typically do not contain or separate out information on university center students. As more and better data become available, there are four research areas with high potential value.

- National status studies—The difficulty experienced in finding definitive background information for this chapter exemplifies the need for national status studies. Ideally, future research would focus on student profiles and demographic information, the nature and extent of academic programming, and methods to fund university center startup and operations.

- Transfer rates—Considerable research exists on community college transfer rates and the means to improve them. Researchers should now look to see if the presence of a university center on a community college campus increases transfer rates.

- Persistence and degree completion—Previous research has shown that baccalaureate aspirants who begin their studies at a community college are significantly less likely to persist, or take longer to complete their degree programs, than students who begin at a four-year institution. This phenomenon remains constant even when one controls for variables such as educational goal and secondary school achievement. Researchers should see whether students who go on to university centers have improved patterns of persistence and/or require less time to complete four-year degrees in comparison to students who use other transfer mechanisms.

- Minority and at-risk student success—Finally, can university centers improve minority or at-risk students' rates of success? In theory, the community college campus is a supportive and nurturing environment for collegiate study. Researchers should investigate whether that environment can extend support beyond the associate degree level and improve retention and success rates for minority students enrolling at on-campus university centers.

References

About University of Houston–Victoria. (n.d.). Retrieved July 27, 2003, from the University of Houston–Victoria Web site. www.uhv.edu/about/history.htm

About Us—Universities Center at Dallas. (n.d.). Retrieved June 16, 2003, from the Universities Center at Dallas Web site. www.ucddowntown.org/AboutUs.asp

Argetsinger, A. (July 17, 2003). Demand may outpace Virginia public college's growth. [Electronic version]. *Washington Post,* p. B01. Retrieved July 18, 2003, from www.washingtonpost.com.

Brophy, B. (September 11, 2000). Is a four-year degree from a two-year school right for you? *U.S. News & World Report.* Retrieved June 8, 2003, from the Community College Baccalaureate Association Web site. accbd.org/articles/00000005.htm

Cejda, B. (1999). The role of the community college in baccalaureate attainment at a private liberal arts college. *Community College Review, 27*(1), 1–12. Retrieved June 6, 2003, from WilsonSelectPlus database.

Champagne, J., & Barrett, P. (2003). *University centers: A comparative synopsis and selected interviews.* Unpublished study.

Cohen, A., & Brawer, F. (2002). *The American community college.* 4th ed. (pp. 246–251). San Francisco: Jossey-Bass.

Community college alliance provides bachelor degree opportunities. (October 1, 2002). *Distance Education Report, 6*(19), 4.

Cook, A. (February, 2000). *Community college baccalaureate degrees: A delivery model for the future?* Policy paper. Denver, CO: Education Commission of the States.

Evelyn, J. (April 11, 2003). Making waves in Miami: A leading community college offers bachelor's degrees, reflecting national tension between 2- and 4-year sectors. [Electronic version]. *Chronicle of Higher Education, 49*(31), A34. Retrieved June 10, 2003, from chronicle.com/government

Fitzgerald, R. (2000). *College Quality and the Earnings of Recent College Graduates.* (NCES Publication No. 2000-043). Washington, DC: U.S. Department of Education.

Haynes, V. D. (September 11, 2001). More community colleges push to offer bachelor's degrees. [Electronic version]. *Chicago Tribune,* p. K6909. Retrieved June 8, 2003, from www.chicago.tribune.com

Higher Learning Commission. (2000). *Baccalaureate education in the community college setting.* Task Force Meeting Report, October 31–November 1, 2000. Chicago: North Central Association of Colleges and Schools.

Jadallah, E. (1994). The community education center: A model for school-university partnerships. *American Secondary Education, 22*(4), 23–27.

Kanter, R. M. (1994). Collaborative advantage: The art of alliances. *Harvard Business Review, 72*(4), 96–108.

Kent, E. (July 9, 2002). Programs to promote articulation. *Community College Times.* Retrieved June 5, 2003, from www.aacc.nche.edu

Knoell, D. M. (1990). Guidelines for transfer and articulation. *Community, Technical, and Junior College Journal,* 61, 38–41.

Lorenzo, A. (1989). *The Macomb plan: Expanding a community's access to higher education.* Warren, MI: Macomb Community College.

Neal, D. (Ed.) (1988). *Consortia and interinstitutional cooperation.* New York: American Council on Education.

Our history. (n.d.). Retrieved July 27, 2003, from the University Center of Greenville Web site. www.greenville.org/history.htm

Overview: The issue at a glance. (n.d.). Retrieved June 1, 2003, from the Public Agenda Web site. www.publicagenda.org/issues/overview.cfm? issue_type=higher_education

Patterson, F. (1974). *Colleges in consort.* San Francisco: Jossey-Bass.

Prather, J., & Carlson, C. (1994). When four-year and community colleges cooperate: Studies in planning for enrollment maximization. *Journal of Applied Research in the Community College,* 1(2), 129–142.

President's commission on higher education. (1947). Washington, DC: United States Printing Office.

Pritzen, J. (1988). Academic programs. In D.C. Neal (Ed.), *Consortia and institutional cooperation* (p. 46). New York: American Council on Education.

Quigley, M., & Bailey, T. (2003). *Community college movement in perspective: Teachers college responds to the Truman commission.* Lanham, MD: Scarecrow Press, Inc.

Record number of CCA students graduate. (n.d.). Retrieved July 27, 2003, from the "What's New" section of Franklin University's Community College Alliance Web site. virtual.franklin.edu/1728.cfm

Smith, A., Opp, R., Armstrong, R., Stewart, G., & Isaacson, R. (1999). Community college consortia: An overview. *Community College Journal of Research and Practice,* 23, 371–385.

Truman, H. S. (1946). Letter appointing members to the National Commission on Higher Education. *Public Papers of the Presidents.* Retrieved June 6, 2003, from www.trumanlibrary.org/publicpapers/index

U.S. Department of Education. (2000). *High school and beyond longitudinal study of 1980: Postsecondary education transcript study* [Data file]. Washington, DC: National Center for Education Statistics.

Windham, P., Perkins, G., & Rogers, J. (2001). Concurrent-use campuses: Part of the new definition of access. *Community College Review,* 29(3), 39–55.

6

APPLIED AND WORKFORCE BACCALAUREATES

Kenneth P. Walker and Deborah L. Floyd

The dominant competitive weapons
of the twenty-first century will be the
education and skills of the workforce.
—*Thurow, 1998, p. 233*

Educators and employers go hand in hand, although they are not always in step. Sometimes one is ahead, sometimes the other, but ultimately they need to coordinate their moves, or they—and the economy—suffer the consequences. Educators and employers are two halves of a whole: Without the existence of education, employers have no pool of workers from which to hire; without employers to provide jobs, education has limited purpose.

Among all forms of education in the United States, none is more fluid and responsive to the economy than the community college. When employers' needs change, and when they must have employees who have been trained in new ways, they first turn to the community college. No American educational institution is more able to respond, and by its very mission is even *required* to respond, than the community college.

We are in the middle of the emergence of a "new economy," based on the rapid-fire demands of global information, which necessitates new forms of preparation and new credentials. Employers are asking educators to be responsive to this changing economy and to work with them to provide the appropriate workforce, while educational institutions are struggling to redefine their roles. What should community colleges be doing to redefine their roles? Should they go as far as designing new degrees, including an applied workforce baccalaureate to satisfy these demands?

U.S. community colleges have made their mark by providing open access to high-quality higher education. At each stage of development, they have adapted, added, or merged programs and services to suit changing communities (Walker, 2001). As communities demand more and better educational opportunities, colleges should design and offer new programs and services that meet workforce needs (Walker & Zeiss, 2001).

This chapter focuses on one type of baccalaureate being implemented—the applied or workforce baccalaureate degree—and how it is reinventing the community college, especially in the United States. The first section of this chapter defines the applied workforce baccalaureate. The second discusses the rationale for this degree. The third part gives examples of U.S. applied workforce baccalaureate degrees. And, finally this chapter addresses a call for action especially related to issues of policy and research.

The Applied and Workforce Baccalaureate

As the national and international economy evolves, people entering the job market—the most urgent consumers of education and training—will demand more opportunities to learn skills and to earn certifications and degrees that demonstrate skills learned. At the same time, many of these consumers have limited time for education. They may, for instance, own homes, be raising families, and have full-time jobs; earning a degree at a local community college may be their only viable educational option. An applied baccalaureate degree would allow them to work in the field that they are studying and apply what they are learning to real-world situations while they earn a salary. This degree is intended to fill a growing need for graduates who are already trained, both in "soft" skills, such as communication and critical thinking, and in "hard" technical skills.

An applied baccalaureate is different from the traditional baccalaureate in that the former uses applied and contextual learning methods, and significant learning on the job, while the latter depends principally on academic pedagogy. By collaborating closely with employers, the community college can develop a curriculum that is relevant and immediately applicable to current and emergent needs, especially those that require a baccalaureate degree for entry or advancement within that profession. Applied and workforce baccalaureate programming emphasizes that students apply what they are learning to real situations through simulations and case studies. Theory is less important than "hands-on learning," to the ultimate benefit of employers and the economy.

Some applied baccalaureate degrees have an inverted structure, with technical and discipline courses in the lower division and general education courses in the upper levels. This permits employers to hire students before they have completed their baccalaureate degree and allows students to gain a deeper understanding of their discipline through on-the-job training, as well as to subsidize the cost of their degree.

Because there is great variation among baccalaureate degrees and the major areas of focus, it is not possible to provide a single definition to describe all of them. Nevertheless, we can delineate some general types and their differing criteria. Traditional and applied baccalaureates differ in a number of features: the characteristics of intended students; the way in which curricula are formed; the intensity or diffusion of focus of the major; an attitude about the relationship between the theoretical and the applied and the importance thereof; the independence of the college from its community; the targeting of the baccalaureate to local workforce conditions; and methods of teaching and learning.

The concept of a workforce-related baccalaureate ties student learning and outcomes back to the economic or workforce conditions of a geographical area. It offers the student knowledge and skills required for the local workforce. As the needs for specific skills change or disappear, the curriculum and focus of an applied or workforce-related baccalaureate changes.

The workforce baccalaureate involves a different way of related theory and practice than does the traditional baccalaureate. In the applied workforce baccalaureate, learning begins as an outgrowth of practical problems and situations and progresses, depending on the intensity of focus, toward more general knowledge.

Methods of learning are as important as curriculum design and must also be effectively performed, not only because of the end-point of employment, but also because of students' life-conditions. It must take place while a student carries out daily work and family obligations, in units and sequences compatible with the pace thus allowed.

The length of the "four-year" degree adapts to the student's time and practical ability to traverse the curriculum.

These considerations bring to light a further difference between traditional and applied workforce baccalaureates. While the traditional baccalaureate can be fully successful without any external connection with the workforce, the applied baccalaureate succeeds only if those holding the degree find work in the area of identified need. So the final distinction is that workforce-related baccalaureates are externally stimulated, guided, and evaluated; the learning experience itself fully satisfies the goals of traditional baccalaureates.

Rationale for Applied Workforce Baccalaureate Degrees

According to Hecker (2001) in 2010, 21.8 percent of the jobs in the United States will require a bachelor's degree or higher. The U.S. Department of Labor's study "Tomorrow's Jobs" projects that employment opportunities requiring a bachelor's degree will increase by 22 percent, and those requiring an associate degree, by 32 percent (U.S. Department of Labor, Bureau of Labor Statistics, 2003). Because the growth and demand for baccalaureates is being fueled so much by specific workplace needs, it is highly possible that in addition to the demand for traditional baccalaureates there will be a growing demand for baccalaureates that are focused on specific workplace skills.

Increasingly, the employment marketplace will reward people who hold both occupational skill certifications and associate or applied bachelor's degrees (Kaihla, 2003). Applied degrees are preferable in advanced technologies, but associate degrees are adequate for entry-level technology positions. Convenient access to skills training, leading to certification or degrees if desired, is critical to students and for the economy.

Another factor which is contributing to the interest in the applied workforce baccalaureate is globalization. Garmon (2003) argues that the United States can become more competitive in international markets by producing highly skilled and credentialed workers. Globalization itself creates pressure for a new kind of delivery system for workplace skills.

Acquiring an applied workforce baccalaureate degree may be a profitable strategy for job seekers in today's highly competitive labor markets. In the late 1990s, when employers were desperate for skilled technical workers—it was a "sellers' market"—job seekers needed no more than an industry-recognized certification to land a good position. In today's economy—a "buyers' market"—employers can be more selective; they prefer a combination of an associate or bachelor's degree (preferably an applied or technical degree, although liberal arts degrees are also acceptable) and an appropriate certificate (Wyrostek, 2001).

Applied Workforce Baccalaureate Degrees—United States

One might argue that a major reason for approval of community colleges' proposals to confer baccalaureate degrees is that the degrees proposed meet an identified workforce need. For example, the 2002 Florida Board of Education's action supporting community college baccalaureate degrees emphasized that the degrees proposed must meet an identified unmet need in the workforce. Most recently, the Texas Coordinating Board approved three community colleges to confer baccalaureate degrees, again to meet unmet workforce needs (Wertheimer, 2003). In Hawaii, three community colleges were approved to offer baccalaureate degrees, all in workforce-related areas (Patton, 2003).

For the purposes of this chapter we will define applied workforce baccalaureate degrees as those which have been specifically created to meet identified workforce demands such as teacher education and certification, nursing, culinary arts, electronic technology, information systems technology, computing, and business administration.

Recently there have been numerous reports in the media of new baccalaureate programs in many states which, from the titles of the programs, sound as if they are workforce baccalaureates. Often these reports fail to indicate precisely where the programs are in the development–implementation process. Thus, it is impossible to provide a precise listing of all workforce baccalaureate programs that presently are being offered in United States community colleges. However, we can provide examples of developments in some states based on our criteria for defining an applied workforce baccalaureate degree.

In Chapter 7, Thomas E. Furlong, Jr. describes in detail how St. Petersburg College in Florida developed baccalaureate degrees and gained approval, including the language of the Florida legislation that requires that these community college programs meet workforce needs. St. Petersburg's workforce baccalaureate program areas include nursing, teacher education, technology management, and dental hygiene, and they are planning other programs such as orthodontics and prosthetics. Other Florida community colleges that have been approved to confer baccalaureate degrees have also focused on workforce needs in areas of teacher education (Miami-Dade), project and acquisitions management (Okaloosa Walton), and teacher education (Chipola).

The three Texas community colleges approved to develop baccalaureate degree programs also are in areas of workforce needs. Brazosport College, Midland College, and South Texas Community College were approved by the Texas Coordinating Board to develop applied baccalaureate degree programs as a pilot project. "All three schools want to offer degrees in applied science and technology fields that correspond to the needs of industries near their campuses." (Wertheimer, 2003, p. 1B & 4B).

Three of Hawaii's community colleges have been authorized by their board of regents to plan baccalaureate programs in areas of business and information technology, computer electronic technology and culinary arts (Patton, 2003).

In Chapter 9, Ron and Nancy Remington described the development of the bachelor of arts in elementary education at Great Basin College (GBC) in Nevada. GBC also is developing baccalaureate degree programs in areas of nursing and integrative professional studies and applied science.

Barbara K. Townsend's Chapter 11 and Deborah L. Floyd's Chapter 3 both include descriptions of community college baccalaureate programs in other states that may be regarded as workforce baccalaureates.

Issues for Policy and Research

Policy Issues

- States need to develop frameworks and criteria for granting the authority to community colleges to offer applied workforce baccalaureate degrees.

- Given the difference between applied workforce baccalaureate and traditional baccalaureate degrees, an important question is whether the applied degrees would be recognized by universities for admission to graduate programs.

- In view of the applied emphasis in the workforce baccalaureate programs, consideration needs to be given to whether traditional faculty qualifications and work loads are appropriate for these new degree areas.

Research Issues

- It would be important to study how accreditation criteria and processes are applied to community colleges pursuing workforce baccalaureate degree approval.

- Given recent trends toward certification of skills and knowledge in information technology and other areas of developing technology, research is needed on how to relate degree recognition with skill and knowledge certification.

Call for Action—Concluding Comment

Community colleges have a rich history of responsiveness to their communities. Meeting the growing demands by students and employers for a higher level of workforce-related knowledge and skill is a logical next step for community colleges. Baccalaureate degrees are increasingly becoming a credential required for the better paying and more secure jobs, often in workforce-related disciplines. Therefore, community colleges are perfectly positioned to embrace the challenges of the future which may result in a different way of programming and include applied workforce baccalaureate degrees.

References

Garmon, J. (2003). Closing the degree divide. *ACCBD* Web site. Retrieved September 15, 2003, from www.accbd.org/articles.htm
Hecker, D. (2001). Occupational employment projections to 2010. *Monthly Labor Review, 124*(11), 83.

Kaihla, P. (September, 2003). The coming job boom. *Business 2.0, 4,* 97–104.

Patton, M. (May 27, 2003). University of Hawaii reorganizes community colleges. *Community College Times,* 15(11), 10.

Thurow, L. (1998). Changing the nature of capitalism. In R. Gibson (Ed.), *Rethinking the future* (pp. 145–233). London: Nicholas Brealey Publishing, Ltd.

U.S. Department of Labor, Bureau of Labor Statistics (2003). *Occupational Outlook Handbook,* 3.

Walker, K. P. (2001). An open door to the bachelor's degree. *Leadership Abstracts, 4,* 2. Retrieved September 15, 2003, from *www.accbd.org/articles.htm*

Walker, K. P., & Zeiss, T. (2001). Design for change: Degrees and skills. *AACC Journal, 71,* 3, 8–18.

Wertheimer, L. K. (July 19, 2003). Three Texas community colleges to grant bachelor's degrees. *Dallas Morning News,* b1& b5.

Wyrostek, W. (2001). Now what? A case for certification. *Information Technology Association of America.* Retrieved from www.informit.com

7

ST. PETERSBURG COLLEGE

INCREASING BACCALAUREATE ACCESS
IN CRITICAL PROGRAM AREAS

Thomas E. Furlong, Jr.

St. Petersburg College (SPC), Florida's oldest two-year community college, celebrated its seventy-fifth anniversary in 2003. For several decades, originally as St. Petersburg Junior College, SPC has been a comprehensive community college with a fall enrollment in 2002 of 30,000-plus credit students. While largely a transfer institution, the college also has a large number of allied health, workforce programs, a large remedial program, and the other programs that one would expect to find at an outstanding comprehensive community college. It is located in an area that serves one county of the sixty-seven in Florida—Pinellas County.

In recent studies, the legislature, the Postsecondary Education Planning Commission, and a number of outside consultants identified it as having a unique need for an increase in baccalaureate access. At the time the bill passed in 2001 to convert SPC into a four-year institution, Florida ranked forty-sixth among the 50 U.S. states in baccalaureate access (Florida Board of Education, 2002). This despite the fact that in most measures, several of the Florida community colleges were in the top 10 in the production of Associate in Arts and Associate in Science graduates and Florida is the fourth largest state. Among the counties in Florida, Pinellas ranks 67 of 67 in terms of baccalaureate access.

As the Florida legislature began to explore the need to do something to increase this access for the good of local citizens as well as for the ability of local corporations to identify a trained workforce, a number of initiatives were addressed. Both the State Board of Community Colleges' master plan for the Community College System of Florida and the master plan for postsecondary education developed by the Postsecondary Education Planning Commission recommended an increase in online education as one method to increase postsecondary access. SPC embraced that initiative and indeed now ranks number one among the community colleges and universities in Florida, both in online courses and in online students enrolled.

In addition, the legislature also identified the need to have an increased number of baccalaureate programs accredited and offered by other accredited partner colleges and universities on community college campuses (the most geographically accessible campuses) as a method to address baccalaureate access. SPC accepted this challenge and, in the year 2000, created the University Partnership Center (UPC). The UPC has grown to be one of the largest partnership models in the country. The center now has 62 bachelor's, master's, and doctoral programs from 14 partner institutions—public and private—in and outside Florida, with the programs being offered on the six campuses of SPC in Pinellas County. The legislature funded the college to be a host to these institutions and enabled SPC to provide student services, counseling, marketing, online development support, and a number of partnership support functions to these partners. There are now over 4,000 students in the partnership programs, and the center in 2003 added the University of Florida's Doctor of Pharmacy degree and its dental program, which will begin in Fall 2004. This program has been so successful that the University of Florida has decided to build on SPC's Seminole Campus. Clearly, the college has identified the UPC as its model of choice to increase access in traditional programs such as psychology, anthropology, and sociology. Starting with the University of South Florida (USF), its local university partner, it has fully embraced this model, which will continue to grow.

The legislature, in its discussions and studies (and ultimately in the bill that passed in 2001), decided that there was a need for SPC to offer a few niche baccalaureate degrees directly. To offer such programs the college would need to seek substantive change approval from the Commission on Colleges of the Southern Association of Colleges and Schools (SACS). Prior to the 2001 legislature, there were a number of community colleges discussing this option of providing niche baccalaureates, and the legislature decided to take a two-pronged approach in response. One approach was to establish SPC as a pilot to address the possibility of creating a full upper division with supporting infrastructure and a full, substantive change with its accrediting organization. In addition, for future colleges interested in this option, the second half of the legislation provided a method whereby individual community colleges could identify local need and then work with the state agencies involved to seek funding to add individual programs one at a time. In the last few years, Miami-Dade Community College, Chipola Community College, and Okaloosa-Walton Community College have used this vehicle to seek programs and indeed have been approved. Miami-Dade began a College of Education in Fall 2003 and Chipola and Okaloosa-Walton are planning to begin courses in Fall 2004. One other option considered by the legislature to increase baccalaureate access was to offer more support, programmatic and financial, to local, branch campuses of state universities. In the case of the USF campus in St. Petersburg, recently renamed the University of South Florida, St. Petersburg, it had a number of programs in place, and the 2001 legislation and appropriations act provided additional support for Pinellas County residents to begin and complete their programs at University of South Florida, St. Petersburg.

This chapter looks at the transformation at SPC, at its new program areas, and at the facilities and amenities that have emerged to respond to the new needs of the college and the community.

Transformation

Partnerships

All four initiatives—partnerships, online education, local branch campuses of state universities, and niche baccalaureates at individual community colleges were based on the large number of Associate of Arts (AA) and Associate of Science (AS) graduates in Florida; the state's low ranking in baccalaureate production; and greater geographical and financial access in areas such as Pinellas County. The community college, which has an established relationship with the community, in our opinion is the most appropriate avenue to increase baccalaureate production.

The partnership model at SPC in general is nothing new. Several of the six large campuses have significant partnerships in place. The college has recently offered the first two years of instruction at the University of South Florida, St. Petersburg campus, in the southern part of the county and lower-division classes in downtown St. Petersburg in the Florida International Museum. The college has recently entered into an international partnership with Russia and the Florida International Museum to bring a series of Russian art exhibits to the St. Petersburg area in the coming years. The newest campus facility under construction at SPC is in the central part of the county and is named the Epicenter. The Epicenter will house both engineering and MBA programs from the USF, SPC's new technology management program. Despite these strong partnership efforts, increased online instruction, and the additional support given the USF, Pinellas County still suffers from lack of baccalaureate access. This large urban county, which sits on a peninsula separated from Tampa, is the most densely populated county in Florida and the least served in terms of baccalaureate production.

Substantive-Change

The 2001 legislature addressed baccalaureate access by authorizing SPC to work with the SACS' Commission on Colleges to become a four-year institution. It specifically authorized the college to begin offering baccalaureate programs directly in high-need areas: in information technology, where the was a shortage of 22,000 trained employees; in nursing, critically short of personnel, where the college is authorized to offer the BSN; and in teacher education, where in the next 10 years there is a projection of a shortage of 162,000 classroom teachers. In 2003, Florida passed a constitutional amendment to limit class sizes in public schools, thus placing an additional burden on finding qualified teachers in the state.

The 2001 legislation specifically authorized the SPC to offer any of the teacher education programs, and the three local school boards identified which majors were most needed. It specifically authorized the BSN after a number of regional and statewide studies identified this as a critical need. And finally, in any area where the college has an Associate of Science degree, it now has the ability to offer a baccalaureate degree either generically across disciplines or in the specific discipline in which it has an AS degree. This latter option resulted from a discussion by the legislature, noting that in recent years over 200 AS degree areas were identified, and statewide panels were convened to attempt to have stronger AS-to-bachelor's degree articulation to increase baccalaureate access.

Despite these efforts, specific articulation agreements similar to the Associate of Arts (AA) to Bachelor of Arts (BA) articulation agreements on the transfer side of the college could be developed only in five AS program areas. While state universities sought to identify generic baccalaureate degrees that would sit on top of the community colleges' AS degrees, their new degrees, such as Bachelor of Independent Studies or Bachelor of Allied Health across all the allied health disciplines, were not really successful. The needs being identified by the professional associations and the graduates of these AS programs were for specific Bachelor of Applied Science (BAS) degrees in areas such as dental hygiene, technology management, cyber security, veterinary technology, and other related areas that were not provided by the state universities or private four-year colleges. The tremendous success of community college AS degrees in addressing workforce needs in Florida also led to the low number of baccalaureates. The AS graduates were just not successful returning to earn bachelor's degrees.

Community College Mission Enhancement

As the legislation passed in the 2001 session, some of the issues facing SPC were how to implement these bachelor's degrees and be true to its historical community college mission of workforce, two-plus-two articulation with state universities, remedial education, and how to continue the trend to the UPC in the traditional baccalaureate areas. How was the college to enhance its open-door mission to embrace baccalaureate education while keeping instruction as a top priority as it moved into the new four-year model? How can SPC best serve its community with four-year bachelor's degrees in high-demand areas? SPC took this challenge very seriously in terms of the people identified to lead the new programs and in terms of working with the existing college infrastructure to understand that, despite these new four-year degrees (available on campus both in the partnership model and directly from the college), the largest number of students at SPC would be traditional community college students. They would begin at the college, which was known for providing a second-chance opportunity, receive strong developmental education and strong general education courses, and leave prepared to transfer to a state university or private college ready for upper-division work.

The new wrinkle was that some students in these programs would decide to take that upper-division work directly at SPC, primarily those AA and AS graduates, to receive a bachelor's degree. However, that number will be a small percentage of the graduates of the college. Strong articulation agreements, as well as partnership agreements with other state universities and community colleges, cannot slip in any way if SPC is going to continue to serve the entire community. And that has been a major focus as SPC has attempted to work specifically to add a few targeted baccalaureate degrees.

The college has taken a position that, because it is a community college serving its community, its adding programs to address a community need—such as baccalaureate access—is an enhancement of its mission and in no way a move away from that mission. The term "community college baccalaureate" is commonly used. This term has many meanings. In some cases the term is applied to a community college offering even just one partnership with a university to make one baccalaureate degree available to its graduates. That is a model widely seen across the country in the last two or three years. In other cases it is a more established partnership center similar to the UPC at SPC. The actual offering of degrees by community colleges does require a substantive change with regional accrediting groups, and that model is much less common. While many times all such models are grouped and written about together, the model where the community college actually does this conversion is seen in only a few colleges and in very few large urban institutions in the country at this time.

The model employed by the SPC and the State of Florida is not one of converting community colleges to four-year colleges, but rather adding baccalaureate degree offerings to the mission of community colleges. The SPC's mission retained the open-door college emphasis while establishing standards for the junior year to assure that the graduates of the two-year programs are prepared and that they will graduate with a fully accredited baccalaureate degree. One of the very first surveys administered by SPC's four-year college team was to work with graduate schools across the state to assure that programs developed by SPC would result in degrees that would transfer into graduate areas such as the Master of Business Administration (MBA), the Master of Science in Nursing (MSN), and other possible graduate degrees. It was critical that SPC's new applied baccalaureate degrees articulate with other institutions.

Implementation Process

In the summer of 2001, the college was fortunate to receive $1 million for planning and developing three new baccalaureate programs in high-demand areas: information technology, nursing, and teacher education. The college hired consultants and worked with the SACS even before the legislation passed to assure that SPC would be prepared to submit a substantive-change document to the Commission on Colleges in Fall 2001. The document was developed with the assistance of consultants, and, beginning in August 2001, the senior vice president for Baccalaureate Programs and University Partnerships was employed by the college to direct both the UPC partnership efforts and the new baccalaureate programs.

The staff of the SPC Baccalaureate Programs office, working with the entire college, set up, as a first step, a college-wide four-year Implementation Task Force that included members from every office at the college. Every office at the college—Financial Aid, Plants and Grounds, Records and Admissions, Student Services, Institutional Advancement, Institutional Research, the College Attorney's Office—would be affected by this four-year effort and all these offices were represented on the task force. Given this college-wide support, a substantive-change document was prepared and submitted to the SACS in October 2001.

In December 2001, the Commission on Colleges of SACS reviewed the submission and approved the substantive change for SPC to begin offering four-year degrees in the fall of 2002. The process of the Commission on Colleges is to follow up this initial action with a site visit during the semester when students are actually beginning their instruction.

Students started classes in the Fall 2002, and the SACS Visiting Team traveled to the college in November. The team reviewed the entire college in terms of each of the criteria contained in the SACS approval process. It consisted entirely of members from four-year colleges and universities. The Commission on Colleges took the position that offering one upper-division course in effect makes an institution a four-year college in terms of meeting the commission's criteria. If the college offers upper-division instruction, the upper-division criteria for accreditation must be met.

St. Petersburg Junior College, as it originally was, embraced that definition, changed its name to St. Petersburg College (SPC)—as was called for in the legislation—and moved in the direction of assuring that the entire college was eligible for four-year status. Specifically, in faculty credentials and other areas that applied to the new four-year programs, the standards were exactly the same as for any state university or private college or university in the southern region. The visit was very productive and helpful for the college. As a result of that visit, the college received an overall commendation for the work it had done on the substantive change, and the substantive change was recommended to the Commission on Colleges and approved by the commission in June 2003.

The only actual recommendation received by the college, as part of this visit and approval process, was that, while SPC was commended on the faculty credentials of the people hired to work with the college's junior class, the level of credentials should be maintained in future faculty hires. The faculty for the senior class was added in Fall 2003, and documentation illustrating these credentials was to be provided. In addition, the college was commended on its institutional-effectiveness approach, but as SPC actually enrolls seniors and as the college has graduates, a report should be submitted to SACS indicating that the fully developed institutional-effectiveness process has been applied.

The process of the Commission on Colleges assisted SPC as it prepared to implement its new programs, and the two recommendations have been implemented. The concept of "one college" became a rallying cry to ensure that the college would not have a four-year college sitting by itself in some unique location, but rather that its support programs and new programs would be spread across the college in a way that made it indeed "one College." A program may be offered at a particular campus, but sections could be offered elsewhere. A counselor may be hired, but the counselor would be assigned to college counseling offices, so that all counselors could be trained to take care of all students—certificate, associate degree, and bachelor's degree seekers. This model of adding staff to existing college offices was followed across the college, and the initial appropriation was expanded and subsequent appropriations were made for junior and senior classes to implement the programs fully. It is a model that the college would strongly recommend to other colleges considering this approach to ensure that a college remains a single college, with one faculty governance organization and a single administrative structure—a single college in every respect.

The college was able to maintain its focus on its mission by frequent communication through a variety of sources such as publications, e-mail, and workshops. Communication became key with six large campuses—there was no way to have too much communication with the various staffs to make sure that everyone understood that the college was maintaining its traditional community college mission while adding to it the baccalaureate mission in response to local needs for specific majors and degrees.

Program Areas of Emphasis

As mentioned, the three areas of baccalaureate emphasis at St. Petersburg College are technology management, nursing, and teacher education. The initial four teacher education programs approved for the college, based on local needs assessments by the three school districts, are elementary education, exceptional child education, secondary mathematics, and secondary science. Another unique aspect of the 2001 legislation was that the college's service area was expanded from Pinellas County to Pasco and Hernando counties to the north. Two-year programs in Pasco and Hernando counties are offered by Pasco-Hernando Community College, the college's strong partner in those two counties. However, in terms of baccalaureate access, SPC now in effect becomes one of Pasco-Hernando Community College's college partners. And in the areas of technology management, nursing, and teacher education,

SPC is able to partner with it and with the local school districts, hospitals, and corporations to offer the programs in a two-plus-two model. All publications and advertising produced in both Pasco and Hernando counties are designed with joint logos depicting both institutions.

The partnership has worked very well. Initially, it was interesting in that community colleges in Florida traditionally remain in their own service areas, defined by the counties that they serve. This model of crossing into other counties was approached very carefully. The two community college presidents had a number of meetings with their administrative staffs. They are now conducting joint advertising and joint promoting of the programs, and all earlier problems have been solved. Pasco-Hernando Community College will have other university partners, including the University of South Florida (USF), with special bachelor's programs needed by their counties. They will encourage a neighboring partner to offer programs on their campuses. SPC is part of that model, and, because it is situated on the border and offers programs in high-demand areas, the partnership is a natural and is working very well. In particular, the AS-to-bachelor's programs will be a natural strength of the collaboration.

Technology Management

The technology management program has been developed under the College of Technology and Management, and led by a dean. The program is positioned as sitting on top of AS degrees in a number of disciplines, including engineering technology, business, networking, cyber security, and a number of other associate of science degrees at the college. Corporate support has been very strong, with local organizations such as Raytheon, Raymond James, Franklin Templeton, and Transition Optical encouraging the college to start this program. They provide co-op and senior project opportunities, serve on advisory committees, and work with curriculum development.

Since its inception, the program is totally online as well as in a blended format. Courses are presented in a specific flexible semester approach of eight weeks (modmesters) to accommodate project managers working in these large corporations. The student demographic for this program is a 38-year-old employee, at an existing corporation, working in an applied area, seeking to enter SPC. Students desire to learn management and communication skills to enhance their career to mid-management and to consider continuing to graduate school and proceeding into senior management. These serious students, who want to advance through the program quickly, may need to take a semester off due to work demands and may prefer the flexible modmester approach, because it allows them to work at an intense level for eight weeks and potentially skip the occasional modmester.

As stated previously, the technology management program offers both an online and a blended format program. Online has been particularly popular with the students, with approximately 60 percent actually taking courses online. It had been originally expected that about 60 percent of the students would select the blended format. The online students are from Pinellas, Pasco, and Hernando counties. As is often the case with online education, it provides flexibility, especially for technology management students who work.

It was anticipated that 75 to 100 technology management students would enroll in Fall 2002. Registration reached 205 in the Fall and 306 by January. The latest development in the program has been, in addition to the generic emphasis, concentrations in networking and engineering technology; and, an additional concentration, or possibly a separate major, in cyber security is being considered. This area of corporate security represents a major employment area for the three local counties and the national firms with headquarters there.

Bachelor of Science in Nursing Program (BSN)

The Bachelor of Science in Nursing (BSN) program has also experienced tremendous success. It is clearly a two-plus-two program. The associate degree nurse must have achieved a Registered Nurse degree (RN) prior to admission. The demographic for this program consists of older students in their 30s who have received an associate degree from SPC in nursing, have gone into the field, and have returned to earn their BSN. These students hope to continue for their MSN or enter management at their current hospital. The hospitals in the area have been particularly excited about this option also as a career-ladder step to encourage nurses to remain in the field. Several of the local hospitals are financing their nurses to earn a BSN. At least one has established the policy of encouraging 40 percent of its two-year nurses to return to receive their bachelor's degree at some point in their career to allow them to move up into management. The initial goal of this program has been to achieve a "substantive change" from the National League for Nursing Accreditation Commission (NLNAC). It has an accredited two-year program with over 450 students and, in February 2004, will receive a visit from the NLNAC to look at two- and four-year programs vis-à-vis full accreditation. The college hired a dean of nursing, who has a doctorate in nursing, and four full-time faculty members, all of whom have their doctorate in nursing. It is currently seeking a fifth in light of the enrollment increases.

The enrollment goal for nursing in Fall 2002 was 50 students; 65 enrolled in the fall, and by January 2003, the number had reached 104. Marketing of the four-year BSN program and the stress on nursing as a profession has resulted in approximately a 20 percent increase in two-year nursing program enrollments. The Associate Degree Nursing (ADN) program has been very popular but had availability both clinically and in classroom. Now there is a waiting list in that program of over a year. The addition of the four-year two-plus-two BSN option has not only resulted in more mid-career growth opportunities for existing nurses with their RN but has built up the two-year program for future RNs as well.

Teacher Education

Teacher education has been a particularly important and challenging program to implement. Secondary science biology, secondary math education, elementary education, and exceptional child education make up the initial offering. This program must be approved by SACS and by the state to ensure that students may become certified teachers on graduation. All 70 courses had to be completed prior to classes beginning. This produced a tremendous workload on the early staff. That phase is completed, the program is implemented, and National Council for Accreditation of Teacher Education (NCATE) accreditation is being sought at the time when the first graduates are finishing.

In Fall 2003, the program approval visit from the Florida Department of Education occurred. The visiting team, consisting of four-year college of education faculty and staff members, went to the college, looked at all the new program facilities, equipment, and faculty credentials, and recommended full approval of the program to the Program Approval Board. Program approval was awarded during a January 2004 special board meeting. This action was important because approval ensured that the first graduates in May 2004 will have the designation of "Florida State Department of Education Program Approval" on their transcripts, thus permitting them to take the Florida Teacher's Certification Exam.

The enrollment goal was 150 students by January 2003, and 175 enrolled. The backlog in the county for future teachers with difficulty getting to other programs has resulted in a significant number of part-time enrollments in the program. Nine full-time faculty members have been hired, and enrollment when seniors began in Fall 2003 had doubled, and continues to grow. Early enrollment for Fall 2004 is ahead of last year with the largest number of students expected to enroll late summer and early Fall 2004. At the time of the program approval visit, local school superintendents and principals repeatedly called this a model K-20 program and commented on the extensive involvement of faculty and staff. They also commended the large number of clinical hours required throughout the entire program. This program has already reached enrollment numbers that exceed several of the public and private colleges of education in the state. The college also anticipates significant growth now that the State Board of Education has given full program approval.

Program Quality

An important point for a new four-year college to address is academic quality. The state authorizing legislation addressed this topic and directed SPC to meet the academic standards of SACS and also the quality standards that apply to all state universities. The college initiated a letter of agreement with the State University System on how to define that specifically and is now working under that letter of agreement. All the State University System academic policies for quality have been adopted, including the degree limit of 120 hours, the acceptance of common prerequisites from community college, transfers to the institution, the common general education core of 36 hours, and the foreign language requirements. The college is also committed to seeking specialized accreditation in addition to SACS whenever that is available—for example, NLNAC and NCATE. The Florida Common Course Numbering System will be utilized, and SPC will participate in the library-automated systems of both the State University System and the Community College System.

Facilities and Amenities

Library

The library is an important quality service areas to support baccalaureate programs, and to ensure that the quality standards were met, two full-time librarians were hired and cross-trained the librarians at the rest of the campuses. The books, periodicals, and online services are provided at all three locations where the programs are housed. In addition, courier service is provided to all campuses on a daily basis. The library participates in the library-automated systems of both the State University System and the Community College System. All academic libraries in Florida allow checkout privileges to SPC students.

Financial Aid

Financial aid is an important area for colleges considering entry into upper-division instruction at an existing community college, not a difficult process as much as it was time consuming. U.S. Department of Education approval is needed for upper-division funding in federal financial aid programs such as PELL and GSL; state programs such as the Florida Lottery Bright Futures program and the Florida Student Assistance Grant, a need-based program; and funding from the Community College Minority Teachers Fund. Amending SPC's local fees to ensure that a financial aid fee is assessed to support upper-division students resulted in significant work in the Financial Aid Office. The needed programs are in place, and students in the upper division are on substantial financial aid and meet the profile of the typical community college demographic, the exception being that they are older than the community college standard age for students.

Counseling and Advising

Student services, counseling, and advising constitutes a particularly important area for accreditation purposes as well as meeting the needs of students in a quality manner. SPC took the position that it would add a full-time counselor in each of the areas in which it adopted new majors, and initially that was done. Each of the counselors was assigned to a different site and then had an assignment of cross-training all the two-and four-year counselors at the college but also serving as the primary reference point for students and counselors with questions about the four-year programs.

Records and Registration

Records and registration receives an additional workload with SPC's transition. Receiving transcripts from transfer students from other colleges and universities, from community college students seeking to transfer into new programs, and from students who are taking a single course in the summer, results in a transcript evaluation process that is much more extensive and time consuming than the normal open-door community college process. One full-time position was added to the records and registration office. This position conducted cross-training and worked with the college to shift the four-year programs to an earlier admissions cycle while it continues the normal community college practice of making admission to two-year programs possible for an extended period of time. SPC enters into a cycle for early admission as potential four-year students are looking at other colleges as well and need to make their decisions well in advance. The three deans for the three program areas work closely with the records and registration staff to make sure that the admissions staff and counseling staff are aware of these requirements.

Enrollment Management

The Enrollment Management Office handles recruitment at the college. It is centrally coordinated with a group of recruiters and a call center operation to ensure that there is one phone number available to students who want to call for information about the college. Two recruiters have been added for the new programs, and they have done extensive information sessions at corporate locations, hospitals, and school districts. The college is working with area community colleges to assure that they are aware of new programs and requirements. The enrollment management staff has met with other community colleges on their college nights to inform the students of those institutions of the possibility of transferring at the junior year to SPC. Fourteen of the twenty-eight community colleges in Florida have approached SPC about serving as one of their college partners in offering online programs at their sites. SPC is seriously looking into this option and currently is in discussion with Broward Community College about making the technology management program available at that institution. This high level of interest is a direct result of the need for articulation of associate-to-bachelor's programs and of the college's unique history making it particularly effective in this area.

Marketing

Marketing has been an important area as the new programs started up. The name changed to St. Petersburg College from St. Petersburg Junior College, the cooperative agreements with Pasco-Hernando Community College and other community colleges were developed, and the need to disseminate information on an earlier admissions cycle became important. A particularly successful marketing method has been direct mailing.

Facilities

Some renovations were made to facilities to serve specific programs, some new facilities were constructed and some portable buildings were used. Since the nursing program requires an RN for admission, the upper division is largely a management and communications set of courses, and there is not extensive need for additional clinical space. The number of students in the program will result in additional classroom needs, and that will be addressed over time. Two of the initial BSN student cohorts are actually taking classes at hospital training sites. Currently the existing Health Education Center is well-able to handle BSN needs and the needs of the upcoming dental hygiene majors.

In terms of capital outlay funding for new programs, the authorizing legislation provided that SPC seek two-year program facility needs through the Florida Community College System and four-year needs through the capital-outlay process of the State University System. The funds for the College of Education building and for the other renovations that have occurred to date have come from the Florida State University System portion of the college's capital-outlay funding formula.

Faculty

Faculty is a particularly important developmental piece of this substantive change at SPC. All four-year faculty members are on the same pay schedule as the lower division SPC faculty. New faculty members have been asked to be on 12-month contracts during this developmental phase to assure that in addition to their teaching loads they are able to provide some administrative support and curriculum design support to the deans as the college grows. One class release time is provided for four-year college faculty members to serve as faculty advisors with the new students, particularly in the light of the placement responsibilities of a four-year college at the end of the program. All faculty hires to date have either their Ph.D. or equivalent in field or have been all but dissertation (ABD) with significant teaching experience. The faculty governance organization at SPC has amended its constitution to provide for new members to become part of that organization to assure one faculty at the college. While research is not directly funded by the state, the college recognizes research efforts as important to quality teaching and seeks ways to publicize research efforts. All promotions and pay adjustments of faculty members, however, are tied to effective teaching.

New Program Possibilities

Some of the initial plans for additional degrees have been discussed in the light of the college's ability to add AS-to-BAS degree programs as needs demand. Dental hygiene, cyber security, public safety management, veterinary technology, and international finance are being discussed. These majors relate either to local needs or to special, documented requests. Dental hygiene, for example, will begin in January 2004. Statewide associations and other community colleges, both in Florida and nationally, asked

SPC to add dental hygiene to provide a faculty resource for existing two-year programs. A significant number of two-year dental hygiene programs have been added around the country in recent years, and yet there has been a decline in the number of bachelor's and master's degree holders in dental hygiene. It is the college's plan that this totally online program will enable additional faculty members to be available to two-year programs nationally. Graduates will also be qualified for pharmaceutical and other dental-related businesses. This program will assume that the applicant has an AS degree, experience, and an existing license as a dental hygienist. SPC will be providing management and communication skills, and students will have the ability to become a teacher/faculty member in dental hygiene as part of the college's plan for this program. Approximately fifty students were anticipated in January 2003; However, over 250 inquiries have been received, and the program will begin with approximately seventy-five students in January 2004.

Public safety management is a four-year major that has been sought by the local fire, police, and emergency-management community. Given both the significant number of associate degree programs at the college in these areas, and the great interest by the public safety community, the Board of Trustees in October 2003 approved public safety as the next degree area. Classes begin in August 2004.

Finally, the area of orthotics and prosthetics is an area with a significant national need and very few programs nationally. The orthotics and prosthetics community, Shriners Hospital, and others in the state and regionally, have approached the college about offering a bachelor's degree in this area, as well as an additional associate's degree and a certificate program. The local university was approached and has deferred to SPC to consider this program. A joint $750,000 fund-raising campaign has been initiated to secure some private money for this costly program. It is a program that is greatly needed and a program the college is very excited about offering. This program is tentatively scheduled for January 2005, and a full-time dean is being sought.

Again, SPC plans to utilize the university partnership model as needs are identified for bachelor's degrees in such traditional areas as psychology, and partners will be invited to offer these important programs on its campuses as part of its UPC. Table 7.1 includes an outline of the college's steps for new four-year program approval.

Table 7.1   St. Petersburg College Process for Consideration
of Additional Baccalaureate Programs

A. Needs assessment

- Student interest (survey)
- Job projections (local, statewide); positions available for graduates
- Current and projected labor market analysis (number of current and needed professionals in field)

B. Costs of Program

- Faculty
- Equipment
- Facilities/Online possibilities
- Other expenses

C. Proposed campus location

D. Projected enrollment

- First year headcount (unduplicated); Full Time Equivalent (FTE)
- Subsequent years

E. Other private/public institutions offering program: local; statewide

F. Differentiation between currently offered programs and SPC's proposed program

G. Potential partners (UPC proposals)

H. Narrative rationale (SPC direct offering)

Finance Formula

The finance formula used to support SPC's four-year programs is an area of significant interest to inquirers about the new programs. The legislature has taken the position that SPC should be able to offer the programs at some savings to taxpayers, since the students are local, and the college does not have the research function of state universities. While the goal of the program was not simply to be a less expensive program, but rather to provide greater access geographically and at a lower cost to students, the concept of providing that at a lower cost to taxpayers is one that has been fully embraced by the college.

The initial formula is calculated with the state university upper-division cost per student minus the research factor received by those upper-division universities. In addition, the legislation provides that the SPC Board of Trustees should adopt fees for the upper-division courses at a point between the community college fee per credit hour and the existing State University System fees. The college chose the mid-point of that range, and when fees increase in the State University System, SPC increases will be at a similar percentage and still maintain a 25 to 30 percent lower charge than state universities for similar programs. Fall 2003 was a significant period for the college because the 700-plus juniors became seniors and the next class of juniors began. SPC reached a point where enrollment doubled, probably for the first and only time. It was significant that the legislature supported both junior enrollment in the 2002 legislative session and the first round of senior enrollment in the 2003 session. Students who trusted the college to develop these programs and complete them could finish at SPC as planned.

The Florida legislature has taken that step and fully funded enrollment plans. The college is now anticipating approximately 5 percent growth in enrollment for the next fiscal year, and the Department of Education and the State Board of Education have supported its request for funds to the 2004 legislature. SPC officials will work with the Governor's Office, the State Board, and the legislature to continue the programs that have been started at the college.

Facilitating Factors

Some of the key ingredients leading to early successes at St. Petersburg College have been strong respect for the community college mission, funds received for planning and implementation, and the program majors selected in high-demand areas. President Carl Kuttler assured both the college community and the state that SPC would not lose its community college mission.

The legislature's decision to provide planning money up front of a million dollars helped bring early success. These recurring dollars allowed for planning and the ability to hire initial faculty members who would be in place when the charter students arrived. Senator Don Sullivan, appropriations chair for education, crafted the bill with the leadership of SPC and the State Board of Community Colleges, and provided for these startup funds and the funding method for the future.

Finally, the program majors selected for the college were in high-demand areas, and this was critical. Developing successful new programs in areas such as teacher education, nursing, and technology management, in a largely urban area with demand in those fields, made the job easier in terms of announcing information about programs and attracting students. While community colleges could transition successfully in other environments and in other program areas, depending on their own communities, these high-demand fields made the job significantly more doable.

Outcomes

The major outcome of the program has been expanded baccalaureate access in Pinellas County. This has been influenced by the niche four-year degrees offered directly by SPC, by the expansion of online offerings, by the significant expansion of bachelor's degrees offered on-site by university partners (62 majors by 14 colleges and universities), and finally, by expanded upper-division offerings at the St. Petersburg branch of the University of South Florida (USF). Local news frequently reported the competition possibilities of a USF–St. Petersburg branch and an institution such as SPC. The college has found just the opposite. The USF is on two of its campuses, offering important programs to its area. As program demand increases in Pinellas County for baccalaureates across the board, the college is hopeful that it will have additional partnerships with the USF on its various campus locations, at a saving to taxpayers in both facilities and program costs. However, where there are areas that do not fall within the mission of the USF or where the USF cannot launch a successful program remotely into Pinellas, Pasco, or Hernando counties, SPC has the ability now to offer such programs, as long as they are consistent with the mission of this college.

The USF approached SPC recently in relation to three programs at its College of Education in business education/technology education, where it had made a decision to move to graduate programs only. It asked SPC about taking on these programs in its new College of Education. There are significant numbers of teachers statewide who rely on these programs for recertification purposes, and SPC is currently reviewing them and seriously considering the addition of these three majors. Such cooperative ventures are to be expected in the future. The president of the USF and the president of SPC have agreed on those areas in which SPC will move forward in the next few years. They meet regularly to discuss the progress of the college and plans at the USF to make sure that they both move in a cooperative way to serve area needs.

The addition of the four-year programs has also made the college eligible for federal grants in such program areas as the Fund for the Improvement of Postsecondary Education (FIPSE)—funded teacher education programs. The college secured its first U.S. Department of Education Title III grant to improve the undergraduate experience for all the students at SPC, with particular emphasis on those with the need for developmental support in math, reading, and communications. Successful implementation of this program will help not only the two-year programs but also the four-year programs. The staff of the entire college was significantly involved in the securing of the grant.

The college was also successful in receiving a FIPSE grant to fund its new National Center for Teacher Transformation. The new facility, to be housed at the Tarpon Springs campus of the college, has the goal of seeking information on the latest trends in teacher reform and disseminating that information nationally, statewide, and at the new College of Education. As part of the grant, the college received funding to provide "smart" classrooms in a new facility at Tarpon that can be used both by College of Education students in the new program and by the center. These classrooms will house training programs in such areas as principal in-service training, in partnership with the Florida School District Superintendents Association. In the coming year the center will co-sponsor a series of principal-training workshops in partnership with the association, taking advantage of the new facilities and the new College of Education, as well as the model innovations nationally that are identified by the staff of the new center.

Issues for Policy and Research

Policy Issues

- A major issue facing community colleges that move to offer some baccalaureate programs is how to maintain their commitment to traditional community college values. One of the tactics that St. Petersburg College used to address this issue was to place strong emphasis on communication throughout all of its campuses conveying the message that the college was maintaining its traditional mission while adding baccalaureate programs in response to local needs.

- A challenge confronting community colleges that adopt baccalaureate programs is to avoid fragmentation of the institution into separate baccalaureate and nonbaccalaureate components. St. Petersburg College addressed this challenge by adopting a "one college" policy that emphasized spreading programs and support functions as widely as possible throughout the college. For example, counselors were trained to serve all students in the institution rather than having some specialize in dealing with baccalaureate students.

- One of the matters that community colleges must deal with in establishing their first baccalaureate programs is determining academic standards for those programs. One resource in dealing with this matter is the institution's regional accrediting agency. Another is to select appropriate four-year institutions as models. St. Petersburg College made the decision to adopt the quality standards and relevant academic policies that apply to the Florida State University System, for example with respect to general education and foreign language requirements.

Research Issues

- One of the factors that has limited opportunities for transfer is that many two-year programs are in fields in which there is no directly corresponding baccalaureate program offered by a four-year institution in the same locale, or even in the same state. Some programs of this type were among the first that St. Petersburg College considered for possible development of baccalaureate degrees (i.e., dental hygiene, public safety, orthotics, and prosthetics). It would be helpful if research were undertaken nationally on the numbers of baccalaureate programs by field that use the community college baccalaureate and the other three models outlined in Chapter 3, and examine the relationship between the community college baccalaureate and comparable programs in four-year institutions.

• Earlier in this chapter the funding arrangements for community college baccalaureate programs in Florida were described. It was noted that tuition fee levels for the community college baccalaureate programs were set at the midpoint of the range between the community college fee per credit hour and the fee in the State University System. Research should be undertaken regarding funding approaches and tuition fee levels for community college baccalaureates in other states.

Concluding Comments

Both SPC and area universities may now offer bachelor's degrees, but the niche majors permitted to SPC are those most aligned with its historic community mission. The USF, SPC, Eckerd College, and Pasco-Hernando Community College have all worked very successfully together to assure that this unique transition has been a positive one for the area, and SPC looks forward to continuing this partnership.

The college has hosted a series of visits by higher-education researchers, graduate students, and members of the State Board of Education. The visitors have noted the consistent theme that they observed which includes an understanding that there was a local need identified by both state and local groups. They have reaffirmed what SPC leaders knew—that the college saw the community need and responded to it, and that this was simply an attempt to increase baccalaureate access for residents in specific areas identified by the community.

It is the feeling of the staff of the college, after working with this for the past few years, that partnership is of tremendous value and may well be the model that some colleges embrace as the single model. And some of those colleges will invite SPC in as a partner, with some of its online baccalaureate programs. Institutions such as Miami-Dade Community College have looked at their community and have identified various areas of strength at their college where they feel they can enhance their current mission directly and offer some bachelor's programs under their own accreditation. They have asked SPC to work with them as they develop those programs.

In a rapidly growing and uniquely diverse state such as Florida, it just makes sense that a variety of options would be available to residents who want to earn relevant baccalaureate degrees. As we move into this new century, we are challenged by the realizations that Florida and our communities are ranked relatively low in baccalaureate production and availability. At SPC we have embraced this challenge of providing baccalaureate access by enhancing our mission so we are providing certain relevant baccalaureate degrees to our communities.

References

Florida Board of Education. (February 13, 2002). *Access to baccalaureate degree instruction in Florida: Options and opportunities.* Background paper. Retrieved April 12, 2004 from http://www.flboe.org/meetings/Feb02/AccesstoBacc_paper_02.pdf

8

WESTARK'S WORKFORCE
BACCALAUREATE

Jonathon V. McKee

Westark College in Fort Smith, Arkansas was established in 1928. In 1997, it was granted the authority to offer up to nine bachelor degree programs. At that time, Westark was, as it had long been, a comprehensive community college. On January 1, 2002, it became the University of Arkansas at Fort Smith. This chapter describes the development of the first of Westark's baccalaureate programs, the Bachelor of Manufacturing Technology, which was established in Fall 1998, when Westark was still a community college. Irrespective of the change in the corporate nature of Westark as an institution, what should be of particular interest to community colleges in this case are the process by which the institution's first baccalaureate program was developed, and the unique curriculum design for the program.

The Westark baccalaureate in manufacturing technology was developed to respond to Fort Smith's manufacturing employment needs. Within this degree program there were three primary movements at play. First, and most obvious, this new program involved the community college expanding its mission to include baccalaureate programs. Second, the focal point of the program design was the demonstration of students' mastered competencies. Finally, the program design integrated the general education requirement into the competence-based curriculum. Individually, these threads were relatively innovative. Combining these components into one degree program was an entirely new concept (Evelyn, 1999; Harriman & Thicksten, 1997; McKee, 2001; Trannehill & Conner, 2001).

Westark's workforce baccalaureate was developed through a concentrated effort involving several key stakeholders. A powerful state senator and representative, CEOs from major corporations, students, faculty, and administrators combined forces to initiate, support, and ultimately gain approval for this new degree program. Had this support not been in place it is very likely that this unique bachelor degree program would not have been established (McKee, 2001).

The American community college is arguably the greatest change in higher education since the creation of the modern university. Since the first community college was established approximately 100 years ago, there have been significant stages of development, where the fundamental nature of these institutions has shifted. The community college baccalaureate may represent another major shift in the purpose of the U.S. community college (McKee, 2001).

Community colleges throughout the United States collaborate with four-year institutions to set up local university centers, branch campuses at community colleges, interinstitutional consortia, and two-plus-two partnerships, all with the aim of providing greater access to baccalaureate education. However, as Deborah L. Floyd noted in Chapter 3, the curricular control of these partnerships often remains under the jurisdiction of the four-year institution granting the baccalaureate degree. Unlike these collaborative relationships, the community college baccalaureate degree is under the jurisdiction of the community college granting the degree.

Fort Smith, Arkansas, has a population of 70,000 and a manufacturing employment base of 30,000 workers. For the past 60-plus years, Westark College had worked closely with industry to provide workforce training. The Bachelor of Manufacturing Technology is a further manifestation of the evolution of this relationship (McKee, 2001; Trannehill & Conner, 2001).

Program and Curriculum

The Westark College Bachelor of Manufacturing Technology degree is outcome-based. In order to graduate, each student is required to master outcomes integrated throughout several core competency modules.

Individualized Self-Paced Modules

- Word Processing
- Presentation Graphics
- Database
- Spreadsheets
- Internet
- Critical Thinking

- Decision Making
- Problem Solving
- Ethics
- Time Management
- Professional Development
- Written Communication

Facilitated Group Modules

- Oral Communication
- Public Speaking
- Interpersonal Skills

- Conflict Resolution
- How to Lead Meetings
- Teamwork

Figure 8.1   Leadership Foundation Modules.

Each student works through modules contained in four categories, or "foundations," at his or her own pace. The instructors in the program provide the students with guidance only when necessary (McKee, 2001).

The modules are organized into four foundations. Following the completion of a foundation, each student has to complete a "transfer activity" prior to moving on to the next foundation. In the transfer activity, the student has to demonstrate, through a group activity, a synthesis of the competencies mastered in the foundation just completed. This process is intended to build teamwork and leadership skills while reinforcing the outcomes in the foundation (McKee, 2001).

The first foundation, which is designed to overarch the other three foundations, is "leadership." Figure 8.1 lists the modules in the leadership foundation (McKee, 2001).

Following the leadership foundation and transfer activity, the student can choose which of the other three foundations to complete next: producibility, planning, or production. These three foundations cover the technical competences needed within manufacturing. The curricula in these modules will evolve, as local industries' technical needs and practices change (McKee, 2001).

Once the foundations are completed, the program culminates in what is called a "capstone experience"—a portfolio that quantifies and qualifies each student's entire baccalaureate experience (Evelyn, 1999; McKee, 2001).

As mentioned, three primary themes were behind the development and implementation of the Westark baccalaureate. We look at each of those themes: community support; the integration of general education and industry-specific competencies into student-centered self-paced competence modules; and the provision of the baccalaureate program by a community college. The chapter ends with identification of issues for future research and a conclusion.

Community Support

The baccalaureate program in manufacturing technology was developed through strong collaboration between Westark College and the Manufacturing Executives Association (MEA). Influential elected officials and several chambers of commerce were involved with the establishment of this new program (McKee, 2001).

For instance, representatives of the MEA acted as advisors during the development of the program. Furthermore, each of the MEA companies enrolled students once the program had been established. The MEA membership lobbied legislators as the legislation was under consideration. Moreover, the part-time instructors in the program were hired from MEA companies and represented employers and the college in the creation of program curricula. Finally, all the initial students were employees of MEA companies (McKee, 2001).

These partnerships enabled Westark to glean the salient employment needs of Fort Smith manufacturing companies, as well as the generally agreed-on general education requirements of the Westark faculty. With this information, Westark crafted a curriculum to prepare students specifically for middle-management positions within the Fort Smith manufacturing community. Support developed by the college from a broad range of constituents and the goal of meeting community workforce needs were overarching themes throughout the development of this new program (McKee, 2001)

A Unique Delivery Model

As has been stated, the Westark College Bachelor of Manufacturing Technology degree program consists of a series of self-paced competence-based modules that contain curricula integrating general education and industry-standard competencies. The combining of the community college baccalaureate, integrated general education, and self-paced competence-based curriculum into one degree program concerned the Higher Learning Commission of the North Central Association of Colleges and Schools—Westark's accreditation agency.

Westark had a unique hypothesis concerning the general education requirement for this program, based on the following premise. In a particular discipline, a college may have a group of teachers, and for a variety of reasons even classes with the same prefix and course number may be taught differently. Within these differences, it might be difficult to measure generally agreed-on general education requirements. If a huge diagram of any discipline were created, it might be found that a certain core is taught. Each teacher will have a different variation on how to best help students with general education. Therefore, if a cross-section of teachers were asked what general education requirements are important, there would be a diversity of responses. Where the answers intersect most frequently will provide the common core of agreement. The aggregate of what is generally taught will likely cover only a portion of that common core, say about 65 percent. Then, for the sake of argument, say that longitudinally over five years, students retain only 15 percent of what is taught (McKee, 2001).

Alternatively, start with the 65 percent generally agreed to be the general education requirement. Then teach these requirements in the context of the technical requirements of the applied baccalaureate. Westark believes that this will cause the retention to increase between 20 or 30 percent longitudinally over five years. In Westark's opinion, the net gain is the same as in the more traditional baccalaureate programs, and the purpose of general education is still being met (McKee, 2001).

Working with the 64-member MEA, which represented 200 local manufacturers that employed more than 30,000 people, Westark determined a need for baccalaureate-level education in manufacturing management. To determine the makeup of such a program, Westark contracted with an outside consultant to lead the MEA through a modified DACUM (Developing a Curriculum) process. In January 1997, the consultant met with a group of about twenty individuals representing 16 of the larger manufacturing companies in the area. A modified DACUM was used because Westark had already identified other college programs that seemed to be similar to what the MEA wanted to accomplish (McKee, 2001).

As the manufacturing executives selected for the DACUM process worked through identifying and sequencing appropriate content, it became apparent that leadership was the most important skill set. The executives listed leadership components that they felt were important. They decided that a separate leadership component needed to be up front in the program. They believed that some of their employees already possessed basic leadership skills essential to middle management. Furthermore, they thought that some employees could learn these skills, while others might not be able to do so. Therefore, the executives wanted to screen for leadership ability up front in the program, very much like higher-level math screens for engineering ability in an engineering program. This was intended to "weed out" those people without the ability or motivation to become a leader in a manufacturing company. Therefore, it was decided to include a foundation of leadership skills at the beginning of the program (McKee, 2001).

A 2001 report by the Higher Learning Commission, among other things, helped Westark deal with the transcription of completed modules. Beyond that, the Commission, working with Westark, established guidelines for community colleges under its jurisdiction to develop baccalaureate programs. This in turn may help Westark articulate the baccalaureate program with other community colleges, colleges, and universities. Furthermore, on the basis of Westark's experience with its accreditation agency, any college subject to the same accreditation agency could probably get a good idea of what requirements it would have to meet in order to get a baccalaureate program accredited.

Context: A Community College Baccalaureate

Sparked by the application from Westark for its manufacturing technology baccalaureate program, the Higher Learning Commission produced a report in 2001 that established guidelines for community colleges under its jurisdiction that wished to develop baccalaureate programs (Higher Learning Commission, 2001). Besides being of help to Westark, this report should be helpful to other community colleges not only in developing baccalaureate programs, but also in regard to articulating their baccalaureate programs with other community colleges, colleges, and universities.

Several community colleges are currently considering, or are in the process of, becoming baccalaureate-granting institutions. Westark clearly is a member of this small but growing list. Other community colleges that are developing baccalaureate programs may find it of interest to look at Westark's use of self-paced competence modules and the way in which general education was integrated into those modules; the latter is illustrated in Figure 8.2. This approach could be used in both community college baccalaureate and nonbaccalaureate programs.

Issues for Policy and Research

Several issues emerge from study of the Westark baccalaureate described in this chapter.

- First, before community colleges launch baccalaureate programs they should consider their motivation for doing so. In Westark's case, the motivation was to respond to the needs of local industry. In time, however, policy makers should be aware that governance changes may or may not follow these programming additions.

- Secondly, the way general education programming was integrated with occupational and skill training at Westark may be considered by some as a model workforce baccalaureate worthy of further study.

- As noted by other authors in this book, the fiscal ramifications of community college baccalaureate degrees should be addressed by researchers and policy makers. For example, the community

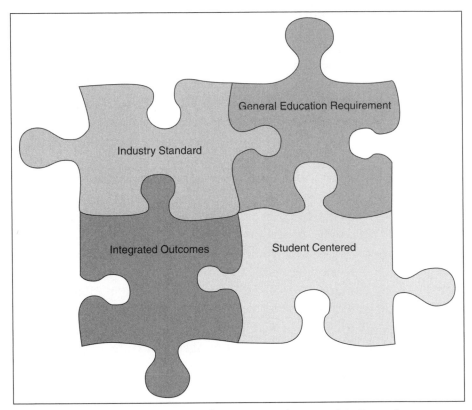

Figure 8.2 Integrated View of Features of Westark's Baccalaureate.

college baccalaureate will require additional resources for such things as enhancing libraries' holdings, laboratories, and possibly faculty salaries and reductions in teaching contact hours. Meeting these added costs may come at the expense of traditional community college programs, although research is needed to describe the fiscal ramifications of this added programming (Campbell, Rosenthal, Wallace, & Wolf, 1998; Cook, 1999).

- Leaders, policy makers, and researchers should continue to deliberate about how to (re)define the new baccalaureate. Accrediting associations, states, local colleges, and others are struggling to develop descriptive criteria and standards that are appropriate for the variety of new forms of baccalaureate programming. As Deborah L. Floyd describes in Chapter 3, a need is evident for clarification of terminology that accurately describes the various models of baccalaureate programming that are connected to community colleges.

Concluding Comments

The Westark College Bachelor of Manufacturing Technology degree program was established as a result of a fusion of three overarching and compelling themes. Those themes were community support towards an initiative to meet community needs; an alternative delivery model; and the baccalaureate degree itself. While it was significant that Westark was offering one baccalaureate program, on closer inspection, the way in which the program and curriculum were delivered may be even more compelling.

Any future study will need to establish what a community college bachelor's degree means. What if the Bachelor of Manufacturing Technology had been named a three-year Associate of Manufacturing Technology? The Fashion Institute of Technology (a community college in New York state) offers several fashion industry-related baccalaureate programs in addition to three-year certificate programs. Might this have been an option for Westark College?

To some extent, the naming of the degree has caused the true nature of the program to be more difficult to discern. Two of the primary elements at play in the Westark program—curricula supporting industry-standard, student-mastered competencies and the integration of general education with these competencies—have far broader implication for higher education. Therefore these forces have the potential for a greater impact on higher education than one baccalaureate program. Essentially, this approach to program planning and curriculum development could be applied to community college certificate and associate degree programs, as well as to university baccalaureate and perhaps even graduate degree programs.

Whether or not the Westark baccalaureate will be unique to Fort Smith, Arkansas, remains to be seen. Other community colleges may attempt to adopt the Westark model. Aligning the social, economic, political, and pedagogical forces to develop a baccalaureate that includes integrated student-mastered competencies could be difficult.

Meanwhile, Westark College has provided a model for other community colleges that may currently, or in the future, be considering a bachelor degree program.

References

Campbell, C., Rosenthal, L., Wallace, S., & Wolf, D. (1998). Policy issue forum: Should community colleges be granted authority to award baccalaureate degrees? Association for Community College Trustees Annual Convention. Audio tape.

Cook, A. (1999). *Community college baccalaureate degrees: A delivery model for the future?* Policy issues paper. Denver, CO: Education Commission of the States.

Evelyn, J. (August 23, 1999). The bid for the bachelor's. *Community College Week*, 11–13.

Harriman, R., & Thicksten, S. (1997). A Bill—Act 971 of 1997. House Bill 2068. State of Arkansas 81st General Assembly.

Higher Learning Commission. (2001). *Baccalaureate education in the community college setting.* Chicago: North Central Association of Colleges and Schools.

McKee, J.V. (2001). *The factors and issues surrounding the development of one community college baccalaureate degree program.* Dissertation at Oregon State University.

Trannehill, D., & Conner, S. (2001). The manufacturing technology baccalaureate degree at Westark College. *CCBA Beacon,* 2(1), 1–2.

9

THE BACCALAUREATE AS AGENT OF CHANGE

GREAT BASIN COLLEGE

Ron Remington and Nancy Remington[1]

Great Basin College (GBC), established in 1967, is the oldest community college in Nevada. It is the major provider of postsecondary education for the central and northeastern part of the state covering more than 45,000 square miles and home to about 86,000 people. The closest four-year institutions are all more than 200 miles away. Because of the nature of its service area, GBC is the state's forerunner in delivering distance education, via the Internet, interactive video, and telecourses. In addition to its Elko campus, GBC has branch campuses in Ely and Winnemucca and satellite centers in Battle Mountain, Carlin, Eureka, Jackpot, McDermitt, Owyhee, Wells, and Wendover. GBC provides a wide range of educational opportunities, including university transfer courses, occupational and technical studies, developmental courses, community education, continuing education, and, most recently, selected baccalaureate programs.

In 1999, GBC became the first community college in Nevada to receive approval to offer a baccalaureate degree, the Bachelor of Arts in Elementary Education. Since then, the college has added baccalaureate degree programs in applied science and integrative and professional studies.

---

[1] The senior author served for 12 years as president of Great Basin College, during the era of the development of the first baccalaureate degree. This chapter is written in first person plural, except where the senior author refers to actions he took while serving as president.

This chapter relates GBC's experience in developing the curriculum and capacity, and obtaining approval to offer its first baccalaureate program. The first part of the chapter describes the background to mid-1998, the second and third parts deal with the intensive effort of 1998–1999, and the fourth looks at events since then. The concluding part of the chapter includes key lessons learned in the process of developing and implementing the Bachelor of Arts in Elementary Education.

Early Days: 1986–1998

Like a venture into unexplored territory, however well conceived, we did not always know exactly what to expect when we started thinking about baccalaureate programs, and we found many surprises along the way. We encountered some smooth highways—ideal for cruise control—but more often side roads, detours, checkpoints, roadblocks, and other obstacles. We had to backtrack several times and look for our compass and a new direction. We also felt a growing sense of commitment: Those of us who just went along for the ride slowly realized that this was the right time, the right place, and the right thing to do. We came to believe that even if we did not receive all the necessary approvals, the work had been worthwhile, the journey not in vain. In many ways, the real learning came through the journey.

As early as 1986, a former president of another Nevada community college had sagely proposed better access to baccalaureate programs for this rural part of the state. As sometimes happens, this notion was tucked away until the college changed leadership. When I arrived at GBC (then Northern Nevada Community College, or NNCC) as president in 1989, several themes led me to try to chart a new course for the college:

- The community of Elko was much too dependent on mining—a boom-or-bust scenario was always looming. Therefore, an obvious challenge for the college was to help support diversification of the local economy.

- The college needed to establish a unique identity for itself in the University and Community College System of Nevada (UCCSN) other than that of the smallest and most remote college in the state.

Although a vision was coming into focus, many obstacles cluttered this road. Historically, the college's emphasis had been on self-interest classes, not on programs, and this created a myriad of barriers that we had to recognize, disassemble, and circumvent.

- The college's nursing program was in danger of losing its accreditation, and serious problems of articulation existed among the system's nursing programs.

- The difficulties in Elko were minor compared to those elsewhere in GBC's region, and the outlying centers needed massive attention.

- The college, because of low enrollment, had no real nucleus of well-qualified, full-time members of faculty, and it lacked a critical mass of degree-seeking students.

With these obstacles in mind, I launched a campaign to stabilize the college for its future, paying particular attention to the needs of the community.

- Within two years the nursing program moved from being deeply troubled to infused with quality. Instructors acquired MS degrees in nursing, and the faculty revised the curriculum and secured accreditation from the National League of Nursing—its self-study is a model for small colleges.

- The outlying centers received new facilities and full-time administrators and faculty members.

- As programs improved, we filled new faculty positions with educators who had appropriate, advanced degrees. On our campus, the University of Nevada–Reno (UNR), began offering master's-cohort programs in educational leadership and in business administration for both GBC faculty members and others in the community who were place-bound.

In 1994, the college received an outstanding commendation in the full-review accreditation process of the Northwest Commission on Colleges and Universities (hereinafter Northwest), and I raised with that body the prospect of baccalaureate degrees, given the college's isolation and remoteness. Advocates for the college, including administrators, instructors, staff members, and advisory- and foundation-board members, met in a retreat in the spring of 1995 to map the direction for the college. They determined to make the institution "a college of first choice rather than a college of last resort" and to improve facilities and expand programs to enhance its image. During the next five years, my leadership team and I steadily nudged the college forward. A series of strategic moves, some concrete and others more abstract, developed the college's capacity to offer baccalaureate programs.

- In addition to enhancing facilities and personnel to bolster the outlying centers, the college launched innovative systems of distance delivery; interactive television and online (Internet) courses have been the most successful.

- In 1995, we polled key players and representatives from the community, and 87 percent favored a name change. Northern Nevada Community College (NNCC) became Great Basin College. This better delineates the region served (northern Nevada typically describes the Reno/Carson area) and avoids confusion with the Northern Nevada Correctional Center (also NNCC)!

- To begin to "broker" higher education in the region and to set the stage for upper-division coursework, we articulated two-plus-two agreements in education with a private college, Sierra Nevada College, and later with UNR in business and then in education.

   During this building phase, I also initiated discussions with major figures across the state, such as the acting dean of education at UNR regarding the two-plus-two arrangement and GBC's need and desire to build its own programs. Additionally, I was in constant touch with our state chancellor about important issues such as the college's name change and our vision of developing baccalaureate programs. Our state UCCSN's Board of Regents representative from this rural area of Nevada was also very instrumental with support.

This background work for transforming the college was somewhat like putting together the pieces of a jigsaw puzzle. A real campus was taking shape, but over a five-year period, other factors and insights allowed us to fine-tune our plans.

- The small community of Ely raised $1 million in less than a year and acquired an $850,000 federal grant to build a new facility adjacent to the high school.

- Winnemucca, whose center had consisted of cast-off modulars, received a like amount from the legislature to build a facility across from its high school.

- On the Elko campus, new facilities included a well-situated child-care center, which replaced a central building with inadequate space and access; a fitness center; a sorely needed small, but state-of-the-art theater; and a health sciences building, primarily to support the nursing program.

- An enormous library expansion, which doubled stack space and tripled study space, greatly facilitated a baccalaureate culture.

- A $4.54-million grant from the Donald W. Reynolds Foundation enhanced the Elko campus. Resulting additions included a solarium, a clock tower, a watercourse, an amphitheater, footbridges, walkways, and outdoor seating areas.

In August 1997, the chancellor and I mounted a campaign to have the state regents support a feasibility study for the GBC baccalaureate and in December 1997, the regents allocated $50,000 for this purpose. In February 1998, the regents chose the Education Alliance from Framingham, Massachusetts, to conduct the feasibility study which included a day-and-a-half in Elko meeting with members of faculty and the Advisory and Foundation boards, school officials, area businesspeople, and elected public officials. The study concluded that there was strong support for the college to offer a baccalaureate program in elementary education to provide teachers for the rural region served by Great Basin College. Following the feasibility study and with support from a district superintendent, the state regents gave the college the green light for baccalaureate programs in general.

Developing a Proposal: June–November 1998

Summer 1998

By the time the regents gave the go-ahead in June 1998, the college had named a lead officer for the initiative, laid the ground work, arranged consultants, and developed a Teacher Preparation Education Partnership Team, consisting of representatives from GBC and the five rural county school districts, administrators, and instructors. The next step was to hold a forum.

A Forum on GBC Baccalaureate Programs was convened in late July, 1998 with approximately fifty participants from the college and the local communities. Representatives from local school districts included superintendents, principals, and teachers. Consultants from four universities were also present. The Forum began with facilitators asking questions, such as: What kind of teacher do we want for rural education? What will be the philosophy/vision/mission of the program? What are the broad-based learning objectives for students? Which courses (general and education) do we want? Specifically what courses will be offered for bachelor degrees? How many special education courses should be included? Is there a way to include middle-school endorsement? Should we include an academic minor? To what extent should this be a field-based program? How will K–12 standards fit into curricular design? As a college, how flexible can we be/should we be, in specific course requirements? How will the first two years relate to GBC's associate degrees? What will be the admission standards for entering teacher education? How can we ensure a collaborative effort? How committed are we to this goal?

The group agreed on basic tenets: early and frequent field experience; solid academic knowledge, particularly in math and science; integration of technology; and understanding the role of the rural teacher. These themes emerged from studying NCATE standards and Nevada Academic Content Standards, as well as some narrative models for teacher education programs—Eastern Oregon State University, Lewis and Clark State College, Loyola University, University of Texas at El Paso, Utah State University, and Western Montana College of the University of Montana. Additionally, certain programmatic themes emerged such as ensuring quality through mentoring; continuous review of programs and elementary education students; providing early and extensive field experience;

fostering teamwork skills and attitudes for elementary teacher candidates; encouraging the values of rural educators, specifically, competency and creativity in multiage, multidiscipline classrooms; and honoring collaboration with school districts and communities.

In August, before the 1998 fall semester began, this Teacher Preparation Education Partnership Team set an agenda for discussing the proposed mission statement, desired teacher competences, and course requirements for the proposed degrees. They spent many hours in discussions and work sessions.

In the search for models, the team found that the El Paso Collaborative for Academic Excellence embodied the principles that they valued. This model is collaboratively designed and managed under joint supervision of university instructors and public school teachers, who act as a clinical faculty; the program takes place often in professional development classrooms; and it integrates technology and effective teaching and emphasizes staff development. Based on collaboration for all entities, on teachers' expertise, and on constant assessment, this model seemed ideal.

Fall 1998

Work on the mission and programmatic aspects of the new degree con tinued in the fall of 1998. On September 24, 1998, GBC submitted a draft of the working documents to their regional accrediting association, Northwest Commission on Colleges and Universities. This was the initial step of its application to offer a baccalaureate in elementary teacher education. The initial accreditation response from Northwest was that GBC had much work to do before the college was ready to submit our substantive-change. The college followed the advice of the regional accrediting association and continued our work on details of the proposals, including hosting more forums for input and advice from a consultant.

Rethinking Everything: November 1998–June 1999

A Major Setback

As advised by the Northwest Commission on Colleges and Universities regional accrediting association, we sent the substantive-change proposal for review to a consultant who offered constructive, yet critical comments. Specificity was needed in areas such as timetables, budget, provision for increased student services workload, equipment needs, and library and information resources.

Interestingly, the consultant suggested that we consider pursuing business administration (rather than elementary education) as our first baccalaureate degree—more easily accredited because it does not require initial external certification or licensure for its practitioners. A year or so later we could submit teacher education. Another alternative was a partnership with UNR to offer the education program jointly, using its faculty and accreditation until we gained our own. Previously, students had been able to obtain a humanities baccalaureate degree, with elementary education teaching certification, from a private college, Sierra Nevada College.

The consultant's suggestions seemed practical and logical but they failed to take into account the situation of students who were in the pipeline counting on finishing their degrees locally. For several years, GBC students had been taking courses in the two-plus-two education program with the intention of transferring to University of Nevada–Reno (UNR). The plan was for UNR to deliver the upper-division courses in the GBC area; however, UNR had not requested next biennium funding for this program and thus, students would not be able to complete their baccalaureate degrees at UNR without traveling to Reno. For Great Basin College to develop and offer the new baccalaureate degree, legislative funding was necessary for start up. The state regents insisted on prior accreditation approval before endorsing the plan and thus, our perception was that this was a catch-22 situation because funding was necessary for initial accreditation and accreditation was necessary for funding.

Back to the Drawing Board

Immediately after receiving the consultant's analysis in November we made a decision to move ahead with our plan for a bachelor's degree in elementary education. We employed another approach for developing this four-year program and subsequent ones that included eight subcommittees, a steering committee, and various stakeholders. These committees reviewed all aspects of the program proposal and made significant modifications in the curriculum model.

We formed an internal Teacher Education Committee, consisting of six academics, to review and fine-tune an admissions handbook and the curriculum for the Teacher Education Program, to prepare for Nevada Department of Education's (NDE) visit in May, to review the substantive-change proposal, and to interview program candidates. We began recruiting faculty and advising students for fall enrollment. During this time, competition for state funding became increasingly intense and intentionally efforts were made to ensure that this program proposal was funded. We continued to forge ahead with the developmental work for this program in spite of the uncertainty about funding.

Coming Together: July 1999–Present

In 1999, the college received good news. Finally, after much work, in March 1999, we submitted a teacher education proposal to the NDE. A review occurred in May 1999 and GBC's elementary education baccalaureate was recommended for approval. In May, the legislature earmarked $1.5 million to fund GBC's baccalaureate program in elementary education. The program formally was granted two-year provisional approval from the NDE in July. Also, during the summer of 1999 the curriculum was approved by the state regents, faculty were hired, and students were recruited and advised.

Since the beginning of this initiative, much had changed. This journey had impacted every department and area of Great Basin College. Adding a baccalaureate program to an existing community college had forced us to rethink most of our policies and procedures. When we started designing this education program, we saw the need to reconceptualize and reconfigure our general education core. This work continued after the summer of 1999, and our goal was to have an "infusion" model ready for our new catalog. We also saw the need for expanded facilities (library, dormitories, and technologically advanced classrooms, study areas, and office space), as well as for services and personnel (academic support, advice, financial aid, distance education, and recruiting).

Although change is necessary for growth, continued learning, and increasing capacity, it is difficult and unsettling. We human beings all have a tendency to resist new ways of thinking because they challenge what we know. It is much easier to fall back on old habits and on what we have done before than to try to envision something entirely new.

So it was with Great Basin College. Although it was tempting to go with a prepackaged curriculum, we resisted the urge. Because of this, everything at GBC changed—well, almost everything. Because GBC is and will continue to be a community college, we must serve our "diverse and changing community by providing an open academic environment where students of all ages and backgrounds can discover their potential and achieve their life goals." Also embedded in this mission is the necessity of collaborating with local and statewide entities for the economic, cultural, intellectual, and recreational enrichment of life here in northeastern Nevada. No other institution did this for us; we had to do it for ourselves.

GBC and the five rural school districts of northeastern Nevada embraced the opportunity to create a new model linking the range of concerns in K–16. In constructing this model, we consulted National Council for Accreditation of Teacher Education (NCATE) Standards, the Nevada Department of Education for licensure, a wide range of programs from other colleges and universities, leaders of neighboring school districts, and other consultants. We consistently incorporated suggestions, state-approved standards, and requirements with what we understand about pedagogy and practice.

We based the curriculum for this program on several assumptions, especially about what teachers ought to know; such as, having a flexible understanding of the subject matter, strong interpersonal communications skills, strong skills in shaping learning of diverse types of students. We felt that teachers ought to be lifelong active learners, and that they should be committed to giving students constructive feedback.

Conclusion: Putting It All on the Line

Perhaps the most important lesson of this journey is that positioning a college for this transition can make it a better learning institution. It is beneficial for a college to reexamine its mission, reenvision its future, reassess its standards and outcomes, create new programs and curricula, develop a new culture, and become more learning-centered. Implementing baccalaureate programs forced us to do all of these things.

In contrast to many universities, interdisciplinary courses will have a permanent residence here. Our faculty members, generally more attuned to working closely with students, are likely to continue doing so in upper-division work. Research will be more practical and applicable to the students' reality. Also, community colleges have an advantage over universities here. They are typically more flexible and less bureaucratic than universities—quicker to respond to the needs of students and employers.

However, it is the students who are the real winners here, as serving students is the true motivating factor with these new baccalaureates. The community college baccalaureate will help students—particularly, nontraditional students—to realize their potential. With so much at stake and so much to gain, how can community colleges not accept this challenge?

Lessons Learned

- Be inclusive; involve both external and internal constituencies in every phase—planning, implementing, and evaluating. Collaboration, however difficult, is essential. Because we involved people from outside the college, they became an integral part of the effort. Because we involved members of faculty and staff from outside elementary education, we bridged the chronic schisms between both upper- and lower-division and technical and academic faculty members.

- Create a program that is tailored to meet the needs of the constituencies that the program is intended to serve. Study exemplary models, but do not just replicate them—one size definitely does not fit all.

- Recognize that an initiative like ours necessarily takes a long time to accomplish. This particular effort took at least five years in preparation.

- Anticipate the new parameters that the baccalaureate will require. Start early to improve faculty credentials, library and resource materials, and support services.

- Invest in a substantial feasibility study to determine whether the college needs to offer baccalaureate programs and if it has the capacity to do so. Do not do anything without such documentation.

- Acknowledge that designing and implementing change are arduous work that will take time away from other tasks. Honoring contributions is essential. College resources will need to be redirected to accommodate change.

- Welcome the opportunity to make your college more efficient and effective, even if that means unexpected and extended effort.

- Persist through difficulties by focusing on the needs of the students.

- Be prepared for constant and unexpected challenges. Problem solving can provide a venue for bringing people together, adding new insights (and sometimes new voices), and infusing energy into the effort.

- Document as much as possible. Turn ideas into reality by writing them down. Agreements, contracts, and catalogs make intentions tangible for those outside the planning process.

- Be tenacious—it takes courage to pioneer a new direction.

- Take responsibility for educational leadership; guard against the familiar thinking and finger pointing so common among educators. Instead, remember that, because of the complexity of our world, we and our students are in the business of change, requiring autonomous, collaborative, and continuous learning, which is the essence of teaching and of learning to teach more effectively. These habits and practices should not end with the implementation of baccalaureate programs but should become an ongoing element of life in the college.

Issues for Policy and Research

- One of the issues facing any community college that is considering getting into offering baccalaureate programs is what program to develop first. As noted earlier, a consultant to GBC suggested starting with a program area other than teacher education because of the complications posed by the regulatory structures for this program area. While recognizing these difficulties, GBC still decided to make the Bachelor of Arts in Elementary Education its first priority because its needs assessment indicated the importance of this area to the community. In this case GBC was able to overcome the obstacles and gain all the necessary approvals, but institutions should appreciate that a bad experience with the first attempt to establish a baccalaureate program could retard the development of other baccalaureate programs. Thus, in deciding where to start, community colleges should balance need for the program with feasibility of getting it implemented.

- Related to the first issue is the fact that the approval process is often more complex for baccalaureate programs than for associate programs. Frequently, baccalaureate programs require approvals from multiple agencies, including professional or occupational regulatory bodies. In such cases, the community college might feel like it is in a catch-22 situation where approval from one agency is dependent upon approval from another and vice-versa. In GBC's case, originally one of its target areas for baccalaureate development was nursing, but because of the complexity of the regulatory environment in that field, this project was put on the back burner. Community colleges need to give careful attention to the sequencing of their applications to different agencies and the monitoring of progress with each agency.

- After much deliberation and consultation, GBC opted for a curriculum model for its bachelor of arts in elementary education that was quite different from those of the university programs with which it was familiar. Given the differences in cultures between two-year and four-year institutions, it is possible that two-year institutions would often attempt to design their baccalaureate programs differently than the corresponding programs in four-year institutions. Community colleges should appreciate that in departing from established conventions for the baccalaureate, they may encounter issues with accreditation agencies. Where baccalaureate programs in the same field are offered by both two-year and four-year institutions, there is a wonderful opportunity for researchers to compare the impacts of different program models and philosophies. Such comparisons would also provide an opportunity to study how institutional culture influences the way that baccalaureate programs are designed and implemented.

- At GBC, the movement into baccalaureate programming grew out of intensive consultation with the institution's various stakeholders. Given the role, mission, and traditions of the community college, this seems like the appropriate approach to take with respect to such a major new direction. Once implementation has taken place, it would be useful for the community college to conduct post hoc research to see if the new baccalaureate programs are actually achieving the intended goals.

10

THE NEW ABDs

APPLIED BACCALAUREATE DEGREES IN ONTARIO

Berta Vigil Laden

Ontario's community college system is among the best in North America.
—Ontario Premier
Mike Harris, 1997

Community colleges in North America are undergoing a paradigm shift in their mission as evidenced by the emergence of the baccalaureate degree in an increasing number of these institutions. Although community colleges continue to be known as postsecondary institutions whose primary mission is teaching and offering transfer preparation and technical/vocational programs leading to certificates, diplomas, and/or associate degrees, they are now moving into a domain once reserved for four-year colleges and universities. As noted in other chapters, community colleges focus on offering baccalaureate degrees in areas with high shortages, such as teacher education (Floyd & Walker, 2003; Townsend & Ignash, 2003) and nursing (Mills, 2003) to address teacher and nursing shortages. As illustrated in Chapter 4, Canadian colleges have concentrated on the creation of applied baccalaureate degree (ABD) programs in specialized technical areas (Levin, 2001b).

The first section of this chapter addresses the shift in community colleges in Ontario towards offering ABDs. It also introduces some relevant insights from a British study. The second section presents the findings of a study of how three Ontario colleges are dealing with funding, program development and facilities, faculty, students, and a changing institutional culture as they begin offering ABDs.

Towards ABDs

The Community College Mission

The research on community colleges tends to underscore the role of these institutions and of the faculty within them as committed individuals who typically spend the majority of their time focused on teaching, preparation for teaching, and course development (Huber, 1998; Outcalt, 2002). American and Canadian researchers (Cohen & Brawer, 1972, 1977, 1984; Dennison & Gallagher, 1986, 1995; Outcalt, 2002; Palmer & Zimbler, 2000) have closely examined the relationship between the community college faculty's development as a distinct profession and its professional practice. From Koos (1924), Eells (1931), and a plethora of other researchers since then, the literature has looked mainly at the mission of the community college as exemplified by the threefold functions of transfer, technical/vocational, and continuing education.

More recent research, however, describes the community college mission as undergoing a paradigm shift, or mission creep (Ward, 2001). Examples of mission creep continue to emerge. For example, vocational education, once considered a terminal preparation to enter the workforce, is now viewed as an increasingly popular pathway to the baccalaureate, as Townsend (2001) demonstrates in her research. Levin (2001a) and others have focused on another paradigm shift, notably the restructuring of the community colleges to offer applied baccalaureate degrees (Levin, 2001b). Canadian colleges in Alberta and British Columbia and now most recently in Ontario have not been immune to the shift to offering degree opportunities for their community college students. The movement in Ontario to offer applied degrees is especially noteworthy, since the history of the Ontario college system is considerably different from that of community colleges in other Canadian jurisdictions or the United States.

Created in 1965 under Progressive Conservative Education Minister William Davis, Ontario's colleges of applied arts and technology (CAATs) were to distinguish themselves from the universities by preparing high school graduates for the middle-level workforce in terminal one-year certificate and two- and three-year diploma programs (Dennison & Gallagher, 1986). A deliberate decision, the transfer function was not included in the Ontario colleges' mandate. Instead, a binary postsecondary system was developed that clearly delineated colleges and universities as distinct and separate pathways to two credentials, the college diploma and the university degree, respectively.

Upward Drift or Blurring the Lines?

Over the past 30 years, universities on both sides of the Canadian–American border have accepted transfer students in increasing numbers from community colleges, and many formal articulation agreements have evolved. Economic pressures and political realities, in large part attributed to a continued migration to a more global economy—referred to by some as globalization (Fisher & Rubenson, 1998; Levin, 2001a)—and increasing funding constraints, have further exacerbated college entrepreneurial practices. Innovative collaborative college-university programs and college-business partnerships have sprung up on many campuses. Certainly, Ontario colleges' efforts to better prepare students for the market as well as respond to the pressures of the business community for highly trained employees have evolved into a wide spectrum of entrepreneurial-transfer and degree-granting partnerships and collaborative skills-based educational programs.

As part of this movement, specialized transfers have occurred due to a new requirement for all registered nurses to have a bachelor's degree. As a result, some colleges and universities have formed several different types of joint programs. The variations of these specialized college-university programs include students taking courses on both the college and the university campuses, university faculty members teaching on the college campus, and students transferring from the college to the university for the third and fourth years of study. Another example of collaboration is the construction of a new university campus on college land to facilitate students' mobility to the university. Efforts such as these have further blurred the lines of the Ontario colleges' original mandate to prepare the non-university-bound population for entry into the workplace. The greatest blurring of that line thus far has resulted from the introduction of applied baccalaureate degrees.

Ontario Colleges

The Ontario colleges differ from the American examples, as noted in other chapters, in that the impetus for applied baccalaureate degrees is credited as coming from the Ministry of Training, Colleges and Universities. When founded in 1965, the colleges were funded almost entirely through government grants and student tuition fees, but by the late 1990s, less than 50 percent of college funding was from the provincial government. Colleges began to seek out innovative partnerships with business and industry in the private sector to help address their funding shortages. The Association of Colleges of Applied Arts and Technology of Ontario (ACAATO) described these partnerships as providing "local solutions to address priorities" (1999, p. 7). Urged by members in both the business sector and in the colleges, and bolstered by the results of various reports, Dianne Cunningham, Conservative Minister of Training, Colleges and Universities, declared that there was a need to "develop a postsecondary education vision that provides the knowledgeable and skilled workforce necessary to advance Ontario's competitiveness in the global economy" (ACAATO, 1999, p. 7). In a consultation paper released in April 2000, the minister provided a summary of new initiatives, including the approval of pilot projects in applied baccalaureate degrees to be offered by the colleges. Cunningham wrote:

> Never before has a good education been as important as it is today. Ontario needs a highly skilled workforce and, with your help, we will ensure our postsecondary education system provides our students with the opportunities they need to succeed in a rapidly changing world. . . . We will continue to rely on our public system to expand the number of postsecondary opportunities for Ontarians. We have been exploring all possible options to increase choices for getting a degree, including some groundbreaking new approaches. The government has made a number of decisions about how to increase access to a broader range of degree opportunities that will provide greater educational choices for Ontario students and promote excellence in our postsecondary institutions. (Ministry of Training, Colleges and Universities, April 2000)

The new provision for colleges to grant applied baccalaureate degrees was touted by both the ministry and the colleges as a move to increase access and choice for students and as a response to the private sector's demand for highly skilled workers with degrees that attest to their higher-level critical thinking skills and preparation. First initiated as a pilot project, two rounds of applications for ABD program offerings were accepted by the Postsecondary Education Quality Assessment Board (PEQAB) from the colleges, with extensive reviews and on-site visits taking place before approval was granted. In March 2002, 12 applied degree programs in 9 colleges were selected. This was followed by another selection of 22 more ABD programs in 16 colleges in November 2002. In all, 7 of the colleges won approval for their proposed programs in both rounds. PEQAB approved a total of 34 programs in 18 colleges in 2002, with some applications still pending until certain clarifications could be made (Ministry of Training, Colleges and Universities, March 2003).

The ministry made two unexpected key decisions: The ABD programs would not be considered "pilot programs" after all; and the colleges could continue to submit proposals for ABD programs at any time, although they would now assume all costs for the application fee and review process. As of Fall 2003, 19 colleges with a total of 38 applied degree programs had been approved, and of these, 11 institutions began offering 22 ABD programs (Ministry of Training, Colleges and Universities, November 2003).

In addition to the historic decision to allow the colleges to grant applied baccalaureate degrees, in February 2003, the provincial government approved the right for four colleges to seek greater diversification in their program offerings. As part of this move, the minister reported that three of the colleges would be known as institutes of technology and advanced learning (ITALs) and could offer up to 15 percent of their course offerings as ABDs. The other colleges would be held to 5 percent maximum of their offerings (for an average of four ABDs each). A fourth college was designated an Institute of University Partnerships and Advanced Studies, with the right to expand its existing college-university partnerships to "bring degree-level learning to the local community" due to the lack of a nearby university (Ministry of Training, Colleges and Universities, February 10, 2003a).

The upward drift to offer ABDs in Ontario has had its share of supporters and opponents. Clearly, among the proponents were the education minister (since replaced after a provincial election brought the Liberals to power in November 2003) and the college presidents. In a press release in February 2003, the minister of Training, Colleges and Universities stated, "Our colleges have demonstrated their ability to deliver new high-quality programs that prepare students for highly skilled jobs in today's economy. By allowing more choice among colleges, we are helping them build on their success and respond to employers' needs for advanced training" (Ministry of Training, Colleges and Universities, February 10, 2003b). College presidents averred that offering the ABDs "is the right thing for Ontario colleges to do" in as much as the colleges' role is to prepare students for the workforce. Since the colleges already offer three-year diploma programs, offering four-year applied degree programs imbued with both theoretically and practically based curriculum and industry internships is considered by supporters a natural extension of what the colleges have been doing for nearly forty years.

Concern about, if not outright criticism of, the new ADB programs focuses on a number of questions. For students: Will business and industry employers view the colleges' ABDs and the university baccalaureate degrees as equivalent degrees? How well will the college ABD graduates be able to compete with university baccalaureate degree graduates in the job market? Will graduates with ABDs be accepted into graduate programs by the universities? For the faculty: Will college faculty members teaching in the ABD programs need higher-level credentials equivalent to university faculty members, namely the doctorate? How will the curriculum be different for ABD programs compared to non-ABD ones? Will faculty members in these programs be required to do research as university professors do? How will the workload be adjusted? How will salary and faculty evaluations for faculty teaching in the applied degree programs differ? Will having faculty members teaching in the applied degree programs versus those who are not teaching in them create a two-tiered stratification system? For the administrators, the questions revolve around how they are to work with the faculty to develop or reinforce the infrastructure and obtain the resources to support the ABD programs.

Learning from the British Polytechnics

The shift in focus from diploma to emphasizing ABDs can have unexpected, perhaps even negative ramifications for the colleges. Ward (2001) states that the shift in emphasis for community colleges is "profound and strike[s] at the very heart of their institutional purpose and culture" and adds that "a course of action that changes institutional identity can be risky, perhaps even fatal, to institutions that stray beyond their well-defined parameters" (p. 4). Specifically, Ward reviewed the changes that occurred in British higher education in the late 1980s and the 1990s when the government granted university status to polytechnics and some colleges. She indicated that similar problems could arise in North American community colleges in their quest to offer baccalaurcate degrees. However, while Ward examined the conversion of all the British polytechnics into universities, the Ontario colleges differ in two ways. First, the provincial policy is explicit that these institutions are still community colleges and do not have to offer ABDs if they do not wish to do so. Second, the colleges may offer only up to 5 percent of their programmatic activity at the ABD level. There are some exceptions, however, as noted earlier in this chapter, that apply to those colleges now known as ITALs, which are allowed to offer up to 15 percent of their programs as ABDs. These distinctions already create a differentiation among the colleges.

Nonetheless, a brief review of the history of the polytechnics' shift to university status offered by Ward (2001) is instructional. The British polytechnics originated at the end of the nineteenth century to teach literacy and practical skills to street urchins. The precursors to the second wave of polytechnics were initially called "colleges of advanced technology" and were established after World War II. In 1966, Labour government policy created multipurpose institutions that offered technical and vocational training to address the growing national needs for a better-trained workforce. Institutional demand to convert to universities began in the 1970s and completed in the 1990s. In her assessment of the upward drift of these institutions, Ward found that the change of name and status has not been totally beneficial to the former polytechnics. Among the adverse changes that Ward found were that the expectations within the polytechnics had expanded. She identified four distinct but overlapping areas of concern in her study: funding, faculty, equity, and identity.

Ward noted that the polytechnics in Britain were at a disadvantage in procuring funding when competing with established universities. As costs for increased instructional programs, faculty salaries, and faculty–student ratios occurred in the British institutions, additional allocations from the government did not materialize. Ward predicted similar funding dilemmas for the North American community colleges offering baccalaureate degrees. In examining the role of faculty, Ward found that while teaching without the doctorate was less of an issue in the British institutions, faculty members were expected to do research. This called for adequate library holdings, proper equipment and supplies, support personnel, and reduced teaching loads—all of which necessitated increased funds for the institutions that were difficult to obtain. Ward noted that equity was a concern, as well, for North American community colleges. Once students are accepted into the British system, they are expected to complete their courses, and so attrition is less of an institutional concern. Attrition and retention rates in North America, however, have been of concern to educators and policy makers for several decades. Thus, Ward cautioned that as opportunities expand for students, equitable mechanisms need to be put in place to ensure that students succeed. Finally, in changing their identity from polytechnics to universities, the newly named institutions found that not only did their new status not rate well when compared to more established degree-granting institutions, they also had to compete in the same arena with the same criteria against these more established institutions. Ward warned that transforming its identity as a community college to a baccalaureate-granting institution could lessen an institution's focus on its fundamental mission and purposes.

Findings and Implications

Research Method and Emerging Themes

This exploratory study reported in this chapter has looked at how Ontario's community colleges are experiencing the changeover to offering the applied baccalaureate degree.[1] The major research question was

---

[1] The author was the researcher who designed this study, collected the data, and completed the analysis.

"What are the issues that colleges are dealing with in implementing ABD programs?"

Using a qualitative approach, procedures advocated by Miles and Huberman (1994) were adopted. The lessons offered by Ward (2001), based on her four categories (funding, faculty, equity, and identity), served as a template for framing the interview questions for the study and for analyzing the data. It was important to determine if the categories that Ward identified would be confirmed in this study and/or if different issues would emerge. Three colleges were selected (referred to as College A, College B, and College C to protect their identities) based on access to them during their startup and implementation. Two were the newly renamed Institutes of Technology and Advanced Learning (ITALs). Data were collected in several ways. Semi-structured interviews were conducted with 16 college administrators (i.e., vice president, dean, department chair, program coordinator) and full-time faculty members involved in the planning and implementation of the ABD programs in the three colleges. Given time constraints for some of the individuals approached, some were interviewed by telephone and others face to face. The interviews were audio-taped and verbatim transcripts were made. Adhering to the principles of Miles and Huberman's data analysis, themes and patterns were searched to be certain that nothing was missed in the data analysis. College documents related to these programs and other archival documents were collected and analyzed. The majority of documents were available through the ministry, PEQAB, and college Web sites.

It is an expectation that this exploratory study will lead to a larger, longitudinal research project on the implementation of the ABD programs in Ontario and that these results will help shape that project. The study is limited due to the small number of colleges and interviews that were conducted by the researcher, and no generalizations are offered about all colleges. Nonetheless, the findings suggest some considerations for further research, policy, and practice.

In examining the data from the three colleges, a number of themes were noted that included Ward's four categories—faculty, funding, identity, equity—as well as students, program development, facilities, and culture. Given that some of the themes were related, they were combined into five categories: funding, program development and facilities, faculty, students, and culture and identity. Funding, however, was an overriding theme that cut across every category, and so it will be described first in general and then as it relates to each of the other four themes.

Funding

First, the findings indicate that while the Ontario colleges prepared over the previous year to offer at least two or three of their ABD programs in Fall 2003, the high costs of putting these programs together, the demand to have at least a minimum number of students for each program offered, and competition with other colleges also offering new ABD programs, led to a scaling down of offerings in the first year. College A began only one of its four approved ABD programs; College B, one of its three; and College C, more ambitious, three of its four. Inadequate funding had an impact on all these decisions.

The financial resources from the provincial government were so small as to be almost insignificant to address the startup needs of these institutions—one-tenth of one point in the funding formula. Everyone interviewed voiced concern over the lack of adequate funding to develop "niche programs" or "niche degrees." "We got no additional funding from the government and all our resources are going toward getting these programs going. Our traditional programs where our strength has always been are suffering," reported one individual. Another stated that "without funding, we cannot develop the way we want, but with funding, development will be quite aggressive." Some colleges addressed the lack of funding by turning to their industry part-ners. One faculty member remarked, "We are lucky that, at least in our field, we have such a strong relationship with industry; however, the funding we receive from them will still not be enough." The frustration in having limited resources was also tied to a comparison with the uni-versities. As one administrator noted, "We have more students coming in just like the universities but we have not been given the same kind of support."

The shared concern about funding, especially when viewed in the aggregate—19 colleges were in different stages of implementing their ABD programs—revealed that no college was alone in its financial woes.

Ward (2001) found in her study that with the introduction of university-level programs in the polytechnics-turned-universities the costs increased in a number of areas while external funding did not match internal demands and needs in the institutions. In sum, for the colleges, the introduction of new ABD programs created huge new expenditures for them that were not covered by funding increases from the ministry. A dreaded outcome anticipated by several college faculty members was that the traditional bread and butter of the colleges, namely, their highly successful diploma programs, might suffer and deteriorate as resources shifted to develop and shore up the ABD programs

Program Development and Facilities

In the call for applications to colleges to develop ABD programs was the explicit demand that they not duplicate any university offerings or create add-ons to existing diploma programs. In fact, the concept of niche programs that met industry needs was highlighted as what should be the distinctive feature of the colleges' new degrees. Members of faculty remarked, however, that the niche programs were "so unique that they did not have corresponding courses or programs elsewhere" and "had limited appeal to students and no viable place in the marketplace." A concern voiced repeatedly was the unknown value of these niche degrees in the marketplace, which would not become clear for some time. Although advisory councils were formed and industry members were actively involved in the development of the ABDs, some administrators were still concerned as to their viability. One individual stated, "The programs that are looking more successful right now are the ones that already had a 'name' program with a broader appeal and the colleges have been able to capitalize on that."

In order to develop curriculum and offer the programs within a year or less of approval by PEQAB, colleges hired experts to assist the faculty, staff, and administration. The costs of hiring outside consultants were reported as "high, yet necessary expenses" if the colleges were to be ready to implement their ABDs by Fall 2003. Courses for at least the first year had to be developed, including detailed course syllabi. The benefits of the yearlong planning highlighted that a "lot of cross-disciplinary and cross-functional fertilization occurred and that was good for all of us, as we do not traditionally use a team base approach," according to a faculty member. The consultants also helped the faculty "marry the practical with the theoretical," as much more theory was required for the degree-level courses. An administrator reported, "The positive outcomes are that we looked at everything and built from our strengths of offering the applied—the real world realities—but we had to think more about theory and how to incorporate it more into the curriculum." The ABD curriculum must include 20 percent liberal arts courses, core courses in the major, and a term of paid internship in industry. A core issue is the increase in offering heavily theory-based courses in addition to the applied, hands-on courses. The internships, not necessarily new to the colleges, provide the opportunity to apply theory and practice in the workplace and prepare students for entry into the market.

Related to offering more theory-based courses was the realization that facilities had to be not only addressed but upgraded, as required by PEQAB's approval process. One of the immediate issues was the need to increase library holdings. Expensive in the best of economic times, this undertaking, administrators noted, requires large amounts of money and will take several years to complete. Another demand is for better-equipped laboratories and more classrooms with appropriate technology in them. Corporate sponsors, who will also offer internships to ABD students, are seen as possible sources of assistance to address these needs. Already some colleges have received contributions from the private sector, but these are seen as only the tip of the iceberg of what is needed for operating the ABD programs successfully.

Clearly, fundamental to program development is adequate funding. As a faculty member stated, "It is difficult to get faculty to deliver a high quality, degree caliber program if they are not really prepared to do so." Bringing in expert consultants, spending huge amounts of time developing courses and the corresponding assignments, and equipping labs and libraries are all costly and essential; however, it was noted that the success of the programs was ultimately up to the instructors in the classrooms. An administrator stated, "We have to be there for them if we really are going to make these degree programs be successful." Ward observed that the reallocation of existing funds, especially when additional public financing was not forthcoming, posed severe problems.

The ABDs introduced new expenditures, which were creating a drain on existing resources. A major concern involves the long-term consequences of shifting support from traditional to ABD programs, especially if traditionally successful certificate and diploma programs decline because they get shortchanged.

Faculty

"Faculty are at the heart and soul of every educational institution" (Ward, 2001, p. 9), and this is just as true with the ABD programs. "Our faculty are of the highest quality and able to offer degree level courses" commented an administrator. Nevertheless, there are several pressing yet unresolved issues pending. One is the workload for the ABD faculty, which is determined through the collective bargaining unit for all the colleges, and the other relates to the credentials of ABD members of faculty.

The workload issue is complex. As the ABD faculty members are expected to offer courses that include much more theory and provide opportunities for students to do applied research projects, they are asking for more preparation time and reduced teaching hours. As of Fall 2003, changes in the collective bargaining agreement had not occurred in a formula that accounts for every minute of weekly contact time. The faculty–student ratio does not appear problematic right now, although the plan is for students to progress through the core courses as a cohort. One administrator, however, was unaware of all the items that were actually "on the table for discussion with the union."

Faculty credentials are always paramount in higher education, as they are crucial in hiring to indicate the level and quality of academic preparation and because they also add prestige to both the faculty and the institution. The issue that arose immediately in the ABD programs was that instructors must hold a degree at least one level higher than the level of programs in which they are teaching. Thus, instructing at the ABD level now requires at least a master's degree—a new hiring requirement. As well, it is expected that "at least 50 percent of the faculty teaching in these programs will have to have a Ph.D. in the discipline they are teaching in." The hiring of new personnel with doctorates was interpreted by faculty members whom I interviewed as meaning that a master's degree is already seen as not enough and that they too must consider seeking terminal degrees.

There are several drawbacks to this expectation. First, the ABD programs are so "niche specific" that the colleges have had difficulty already in finding interested candidates with Ph.D.s in these areas. Second, if these candidates can be found, their salary demands are beyond what the colleges are able to pay. An administrator said, "Our top pay is $76,000 and academic credit is offered only for six years of education. That covers four years for the bachelor's and two for the master's so what does that leave for the doctorate? We are not finding Ph.D.s who will come to work for us with the low salaries we offer. We cannot compete with the universities." Third, as several administrators already learned at the beginning of the fall term, some Ph.D.s who were hired resisted teaching lower-division courses as part of their load. A department chair remarked, "When the faculty member refused, I had no choice but to order him to teach the course. I am afraid we may lose him in the next semester but what could I do? The collective bargaining agreement has not changed and I had the right to make the teaching assignment as needed."

In addition, the expectation that ABD members of faculty will do applied research looms in the near future. There are at least three related issues: Departments must look for external funding for the applied research; faculty members must find time to do the research, despite the workload; and institutions must decide how to reward this component of the workload. "We are already doing applied research so this is nothing new for us as this is part of what we do," stated a program coordinator, "but it is voluntary and the funding is an issue as is the time to do it." Nonetheless, many of those interviewed voiced concerns about this additional area of responsibility for the faculty. "We are not universities so we do not get the money, the time, or the rewards that university faculty do. How will we do research if it is not supported by the collective bargaining agreement and by the funding mechanisms put in place by the college?" asked a faculty member. Others echoed these comments with concern that yet another dilemma related to funding remained unclarified.

Having a faculty with appropriate credentials is important for colleges interested in being baccalaureate-granting institutions. While in U.S. community colleges the master's degree is typically the accepted terminal degree, this has not been the case in Ontario colleges. That requirement is now changing as the ABDs are implemented. One administrator stated that his college president and senior administrators saw this change coming and pushed for faculty development funds to help personnel to upgrade their credentials. An important step was to help create master's and doctoral programs that brought the courses to some of the college campuses or nearby university locations. The drawback to these incentives is that the degree programs are in higher education and the new ABD programs are demanding degrees in disciplinary areas. The faculty constitutes the most expensive part of an institution's budget and of its ancillary costs, such as those for improved facilities and research (Ward, 2001). As one faculty member put it, "the pie is not any bigger than it was before the applied degrees were approved, only more slices in it." College personnel stated that they believe they must compete for resources with the universities to get increased funding. If they do not, the ABD programs stand the chance of becoming second-rate programs with limited prospects.

Students

One of the biggest disappointments noted in the startup of the fall term of the ABD programs was the unexpectedly low number of student applications and enrollments overall, despite the large number of new degree programs and a one-time student phenomenon in Ontario called the double cohort, as the province scrapped the only grade 13 in North America.

The unique aspect of the "niche degrees with a one-term internship" did not seem to attract the numbers anticipated by the colleges. "I think there are so many programs all at once for students to choose from and they are so distinct that we probably are just competing with each other for the same students," suggested an administrator. A faculty member thought that "the niche factor may have been too fuzzy, too vague for most students to understand what they are about. The numbers aren't there."

The double cohort was due to a change in secondary-school completion requirements in the province. Until recently, students hoping to go to university continued for a thirteenth year, to complete Ontario Academic Credits (OACs), and those planning to enter the workplace or go to community college left after grade 12. Grade 12 was revised to accommodate university-bound students, and grade 13 eliminated. The last grade 13 students graduated in June 2003, along with grade 12 students who had also met their OACs under the revised curriculum. Due to the unprecedented number of students anticipated in higher education across the province, there was a great deal of attention given to this by the government, colleges and universities, and the media. For the colleges, it turned out to be "another Y2K event." As one administrator remarked, "The surprise was that it was just flat. We did not benefit at all from the double cohort. No one did in the colleges."

In fact, some colleges suffered enrollment declines, and, although not all the reasons were known immediately, the local outbreak of SARS was blamed for some of the enrollment loss. Many foreign students stayed away from Toronto and the surrounding areas. It is hypothesized that the SARS epidemic that began in March 2003 and lingered in Toronto into the late summer reduced enrollments, especially since students from abroad make up an increasingly higher percentage of the total. Not only do they add to enrollments, but their tuition and fees are also important contributions to the college budgets.

The lowered number of both applications and subsequent enrollees was also attributed to the belief that students who might have considered the ABD programs decided to enroll in university instead when they considered both the tuition costs and admissions requirements. College tuition is set at $2,200 plus ancillary fees, although this can vary by program. Tuition for ABD programs was nearly double in some cases, ranging from $4,000 up to $6,000, plus fees. "With no increase in funding, bursary offerings to students were limited," noted an administrator. While these costs were still lower than university ones, the prospect of entering a new, highly specific ABD program without a successful track record may have proved to be too risky for many potential students. The added element of having to meet substantially higher admission requirements may have helped push some potential students to seek a degree elsewhere.

Not only was access to the ABD programs probably limited by costs and admission requirements, but also an equity issue emerged. The ABDs were touted as opening up access and opportunity to all Ontarians. Yet all applicants had to be new students at the colleges. Students in the diploma programs could not transfer in, as only the first year of the degrees is being offered initially. "It is ironic that after all the problems we have had with universities to accept our students and count the credits they earn with us that we should now be in the same situation internally," said an administrator. Another administrator reported that it would take time to work through all the lateral course transfers and internal bridging for continuing students and that a committee in the college was addressing the policy issue. A faculty member stated, "We need to work on internal course articulation and transfer, true, but it is important to develop the applied degree programs first and get them started before we bring in diploma students."

The marketing of the new programs was left to individual colleges, and the lament by some faculty members and administrators was that the ministry did nothing to help out in this area. One of the program administrators remarked, "Offering anything new requires not only careful planning but careful marketing of the product to the public. It is a costly venture and pressed as we were for funds, this was not done as well as it could have been." Although some colleges managed to get articles in the local newspapers, advertisements in subways and buses, and their Web sites updated, their publicity campaigns may have been affected by the intense media coverage of the double cohort and the SARS epidemic that dominated in spring and summer. Some college individuals stated that the ministry could have made more of a contribution, as they claimed that the call for offering the ABDs came from that source initially.

Clearly, achievements and results of the ABDs are still unknown. Although transfer is not a historic part of the Ontario colleges, the emphasis on providing students with access to postsecondary education and the opportunity to advance academically is very much part of the mission of the colleges. They have provided a pathway for students with partnering universities in the province and elsewhere that have a history of accepting Ontario college graduates. The inequity of raising the admission requirements and blocking out certificate and diploma students is a significant paradigm shift for the colleges. While their intention may be to offer greater opportunities for the workforce, it may be at the expense of their traditional students. Moreover, it is unclear just what retention and student services have been put in place to ensure that the students who do get admitted to the ABD programs indeed remain and succeed.

Culture and Identity

With so much activity involving faculty, staff, and administration; with different committees meeting constantly; and with many decisions being made in many areas of the colleges to prepare for and offer the ABD; the culture and atmosphere within the colleges were in question by some of the participants interviewed. Organizational culture reflects deeply embedded patterns of collective behavior and shared values, assumptions, beliefs, or ideologies that members have about their organization or work, according to Peterson and Spencer (1990). The major features of culture are that it emphasizes the organization's unique or distinctive character, which provides meaning for its members. It is enduring and not malleable, not changed either by cataclysmic events or by slower, long-term events. Atmosphere, in contrast, relates more to current perceptions and attitudes. Its major features are common participant views of organizational phenomena that allow for comparison among groups or over time, current patterns of beliefs and behavior, and its frequent malleability (Peterson & Spencer, 1990).

The mission of the institution can serve as the basis for its culture and identify its purpose. The Ontario colleges were created nearly forty years ago to address the needs of those who sought education and training in the vocational and technical areas. The minister of education, William G. Davis, in introducing the bill in 1965 to the legislature, stated:

> The introduction of this bill provides for the establishment and operation of a system of Colleges of Applied Arts and Technology and I believe this to be a historic occasion in education in our Province. . . . Above all else, it goes far towards making a reality of the promise— indeed, of the stated policy of this government—to provide, thorough

education and training, not only an equality of opportunity to all sectors of our population, but the fullest possible development of each individual to the limit of his ability. In this new age of technological change and invention, also, it is essential to the continued growth and expansion of the economy of our province, and I suggest, of our nation, that adequate facilities be made generally available for the education and training of craftsmen, technicians and technologists. . . . We must and can focus our attention on the design of . . . the applied arts and technology, for full-time and part-time students, in day and in evening courses, within a community, at all socio-economic levels, of all kinds of interests and aptitudes, and at all stages of achievement. (Cited in Watson, 1971, p. 27)

The long-standing mission of the colleges was seen as in danger of being changed, according to some college faculty members and administrators, in the perceived much-too-hurried move to add ABD programs. Several individuals asserted that the minister's push for the ABDs was a shift of their primary mission, as articulated by Davis in 1965. "I think the colleges are moving away from the original purposes— trades and technology. The colleges were meant to support the community and students who could not go to university. Now we are moving out of that into degrees and decreasing some students' options," lamented an administrator.

Another example of a shift in the mission of the colleges was the differentiation between the ABD faculty and the diploma/certificate faculty and the anticipated differences in credentials, salary, and workload. "We are running the risk of creating a two-tier faculty," was a common concern voiced. A more dire prediction was made by another administrator, "If we create a two-tier faculty, it will fracture the culture of the college and change it irrevocably." A faculty member observed, however, that a two-tier or even multitier differentiation already exists between full-time and the various statuses of part-time faculty members, with their differing credentials, salaries, and benefits (or lack of them). "So this is not new, it's just more obvious to more people because they feel it's affecting or could affect them." One administrator, however, stated emphatically, "We are struggling to do the right thing, to not destroy the culture of the college or divide the faculty. We are trying to be as inclusive as possible."

Others noted that the mission remains essentially the same and echoed the words of Walker (2001) that the colleges are just expanding their mission to meet the needs of today's economy. Several people also echoed the minister's sentiment that the colleges had to "think globally but act locally" (October 2003, www.acaato.on.ca/new/swd/charter) in order to better serve the community. These individuals did not see the addition of ABDs as a move away from the mission of the colleges.

If the culture of the colleges was being questioned by some as being in danger, the current atmosphere was highlighted as positive by most of those interviewed. "We have had positive outcomes in looking at everything in the college. We got everyone involved in different committees that we could. We wanted a buy-in from everyone," observed an administrator. A faculty member added, "We relied on our own faculty, some of them teach in universities and have Ph.D.s, to do thorough, rigorous internal review of our curriculum, facilities, skills, and standards. There were a lot of cross-disciplinary committees, something that doesn't always happen. We worked together to create the new programs." Another faculty member stated, "We had lots of synergy with the combination of college and external experts working together that created a higher level mind set."

The issue of identity itself arose only regarding the name change of three colleges to Institutes of Technology and Advanced Learning (ITALs). There were mixed definitions offered as to what the new name meant. The most common offered was that the ITALs were the new polytechnics, "like Ryerson used to be" (the only polytechnic founded in Ontario, which later became a university). An administrator stated that the minister had not been happy with the term "polytechnic" and had preferred to stay away from it while finding the ITAL name a more politically acceptable alternative.

The salience of the name change varied, as well. Definitions among those interviewed varied from a straightforward distinction, "The ITALs can offer up to 15 percent more applied degrees and all the other colleges can offer only up to 5 percent," to "ITALs are the next generation of CAATs and very similar to what has been traditionally known as the polytechnic. There will be a natural evolution to the ITALs." A faculty member noted, "Their definition is still evolving." But an administrator observed, "We have not noticed any differences between the ITALs and CAATs, not yet anyway. I am not sure exactly how it will change, however, the ITALs now have the ability to give more applied degrees and have a stronger commitment to do applied research, which in turn will give our graduates more opportunity to do graduate work." Another administrator observed, "The colleges can still do what the ITALs do. There really is no difference other than in name." Yet another noted, "The ITALs are just a marketing ploy that the presidents pushed. All the colleges were given the option to become an ITAL and only three colleges chose to go in this direction. Our college declined as it had no real implications for program offerings and the students it serves."

Overall, greater concern about preserving the mission of the colleges, protecting the organizational culture, and enhancing the positive climate produced while people worked on the applied degree programs was voiced by college faculty members and administrators. While there was some reaction to the introduction of the ITALs, more overall interest focused on the introduction of the ABD programs and their anticipated impact on the mission of the colleges. Ward (2001) stated that the reason for having a mission is to identify the organization's fundamental purposes and that from that statement it should be clear what an institution is and what it is not. Ward concluded that the true calling of community colleges is to educate and train the "broad spectrum of students who pass through their doors . . . taking those who enroll, preparing them well, and sending them out to be successful in their workplace and in their continued studies." She added that the need for community colleges continues in the new century. "Moving away from their primary mission of providing entry-level opportunities for students who otherwise could not gain access to higher education can only serve to dilute and to confuse this mission and possibly place the entire enterprise in jeopardy" (p. 14).

Issues for Policy and Research

It is still quite early in the implementation stage of the new applied baccalaureate degrees to determine their success or failure. What is clear thus far in this exploratory study with a small number of colleges, is that the ABDs have generated a great deal of organizational excitement and movement in the colleges. Whatever their public or private beliefs, faculty members and administrators have become involved, willingly or not, in a new enterprise that stands to change the colleges dramatically. This particular change has some precedence, as the colleges have been developing other types of institutional offerings, such as different types of college-university partnerships and collaborations, as noted earlier in this chapter.

Policy Issues

- The most critical policy change needed at the provincial level is the need for increased funding from the provincial government. Without additional money, it will be difficult for colleges to market the programs, hire more instructors, improve facilities to meet degree standards, and provide more bursary awards to needy students. More worrisome, resources may continue to shift from diploma and certificate programs to ABD programs, thus harming the former and potentially the latter as well. Insufficient funding could well lead to the quick demise of the ABDs if high-quality programs are not created and maintained to attract and retain students.

- An institutional policy issue that needs greater attention is the ABD curriculum. The curriculum for the second and subsequent years continues to be developed. But funding to hire curriculum experts, to provide instructors with curriculum development opportunities, and to offer them release time to develop the curriculum is essential, according to those interviewed. As a faculty member noted, "Without funding, we cannot develop the way we want to."

- Another institutional policy recommendation is the need for colleges to do outreach and recruitment in the high schools as well as in the greater community to inform potential students of the new ABDs and their viability.

- Regarding employment of graduates of the baccalaureate programs, it is clear, both politically and economically, that the colleges need the private sector to more closely examine the viability of these new degrees in industry and to stress publicly the linkages between them and industry in addressing some of the pressing economic and workplace demands through these new degrees.

Research Issues

- Whether the college mission is truly undergoing a change or not remains to be seen. The organizational culture is rarely changed easily. As Peterson and Spencer (1990) remind us, organizational culture focuses on deeply embedded patterns of behavior, which are not changed by major or by slower, long-term events. The ABDs may indeed lead to a significant paradigm change in the mission of the colleges, or they may just be another example of the continued blurring of the lines between colleges and universities, while not necessarily changing the overall intention and purpose of the colleges.

- How well the ABD programs succeed is crucial to whether there is greater change in the colleges or not. In predicting the future of the ABDs, one of the individuals interviewed stated, "The applied degree will become standard and the diploma will become second class. The students will want the biggest bang for their buck." We shall see if this prognosis will come true.

Concluding Comment

As stated earlier, the minister made a decision to offer the ABDs with the intention to "increase access to a broader range of degree opportunities that will provide greater educational choices for Ontario students and promote excellence in our postsecondary institutions" (Ministry of Training, Colleges and Universities, April 2000). It remains to be seen in the next four to eight years if the minister's decision will yield positive results, as the current and new cohorts enter the ABD programs and progress through them. It may very well be that the colleges' shift to offering ABDs will greatly enhance potential college students' choices by presenting them an upgraded alternative to the vocational and technical preparation that the colleges already excel in. Community colleges have retained their dominance in these areas by continuing to address the needs of their communities and responding to them quickly. The addition of the ABDs in Canada or the baccalaureate degrees in the United States may be another example of the willingness of community colleges once again to respond to greater community demands and to better serve their students. Skolnik (2001) reflected prior to the approval of the ABDs:

> [W]hat should determine the credibility of any proposed degree program is not the historic mandate of the institution which proposes to offer it, but the apparent coherence, quality, integrity, and fitness of purpose of the program itself. This principle is by no means universally accepted, but I believe that in an era when learners are already putting together their own degree programs from a combination of sources, it is on the way to becoming part of the way that we view the degree. And as that happens, the terms community college and baccalaureate will cease to jar the ear when uttered in the same breath. (p. 9)

References

ACAATO. (1999). A new charter for Ontario colleges of applied arts and technology of Ontario: A key discussion of key roles and priorities. Toronto: ACAATO.

Cohen, A. M., & Brawer, F. B. (1972). *Confronting identity: The community college instructor*. Englewood Cliffs, NJ: Prentice-Hall.

Cohen, A. M., & Brawer, F. B. (1977). *The two-year college instructor today*. New York: Holt, Rinehart, and Winston.

Cohen, A. M., & Brawer, F. B. (1984). *The collegiate function of community colleges: Fostering higher learning through curriculum and student transfer*. San Francisco: Jossey-Bass.

Dennison, J., & Gallagher, P. (1986). *Canada's community colleges*. Vancouver: University of British Columbia Press.

Dennison, J., & Gallagher, P. (1995). *Challenge and opportunity*. Vancouver: University of British Columbia Press.

Eells, W. C. (1931). *The junior college*. Boston: Houghton Mifflin.

Fisher, D., & Rubenson, K. (1998). The changing political economy: The private and public lives of Canadian universities. In J. Currie & J. Newson (Eds.), *Universities and globalization: Critical perspectives* (pp. 77–98). London: Sage Publications.

Floyd, D. L., & Walker, D. A. (2003). Community college teacher education: A typology, challenging issues, and state views. *Community College Journal of Research and Practice*, 27(8), 643–663.

Harris, M. (1997). Auto parts manufacturing association annual general meeting. In ACAATO (1999).

Huber, M. T. (1998). *Community college faculty: Issues and problems; a preliminary national appraisal.* Menlo Park, CA: Carnegie Foundation for the Advancement of Teaching.

Koos, L. V. (1924). *The junior college.* (2 vols.) Minneapolis: Research Publications of the University of Minnesota (Education Series, Report No. 5).

Levin, J. S. (2001a). *Globalizing the community college: Strategies for change in the twenty-first century.* New York: Palgrave Publisher.

Levin, J. S. (2001b). *The higher credential: The baccalaureate degree and organizational change in Canada's colleges.* Tucson: Center for the Study of Higher Education, University of Arizona.

Miles, M. B., & Huberman, A. M. (1994). *Qualitative data analysis.* (2nd ed.). Beverly Hills: Sage Publications.

Mills, K. (2003). Community college baccalaureates: Some critics decry the trend as "mission creep." *National Crosstalk,* 1. San Jose, CA: National Center for Public Policy and Higher Education.

Ministry of Training, Colleges and Universities. (2000). *Increasing degree opportunities for Ontarians.* A consultation paper. Retrieved October 27, 2003, from www.edu.gov.ca/eng/document/discussi/degree.html#3

Ministry of Training, Colleges and Universities. (2003a). News release. Eves government expands choice for students, announces new designation for colleges. Retrieved March 25, 2003, from www. mettowas21.edu.gov.on. ca:80/eng/document/nr/03.02/nr0210.html

Ministry of Training, Colleges and Universities. (2003b). News release. Institutes of technology and advanced learning. Retrieved March 25, 2003, from www.mettowas21.edu.gov.on.ca:80/eng/document/nr/03.02/nr0210.html

Ministry of Training, Colleges and Universities. (2003). News release. Eves government proclaims legislation offering more flexibility to colleges, choice to students. Retrieved March 25, 2003, from www.edu.gov.on.ca.eng/document/nr/o3.o3./nr0318.html

Ministry of Training, Colleges and Universities. (2002). News release. Proposed new act will give more opportunities to Ontario students of all ages. Retrieved March 21, 2003, from www.edu.gov.on.ca/eng/ document/nr/02.11/nr1129a.html

Outcalt, C. L. (2002). Toward a professionalized community college professoriate. In C. L. Outcalt (Ed.), *Community college faculty: Characteristics, practices, and challenges. New Directions in Community Colleges,* No. 118, San Francisco: Jossey-Bass, 109–116.

Palmer, J., & Zimbler, L. (2000). *Instructional faculty and staff in public 2-year colleges.* Washington, DC: Office of Educational Research and Improvement, U.S. Department of Education.

Peterson, M. W., & Spencer, M. G. (1990). Understanding academic culture and climate. In W. G. Tierney (Ed.), *Assessing academic climates and cultures. New Directions for Institutional Research*, No. 68. San Francisco: Jossey-Bass Publishers, 3–18.

Skolnik. M. L. (2001). *The community college baccalaureate: Its meaning and implications for the organization of postsecondary education, the mission and character of the community college, and the bachelor's degree.* Paper presented at the First Annual Community College Baccalaureate Association Conference. Orlando, FL.

Townsend, B. K. (2001). Blurring the lines: Transforming terminal education to transfer education. In D. D. Bragg (Ed.), *The new vocationalism in community colleges. New Directions in Community Colleges*, No. 115. San Francisco: Jossey-Bass Publishers, 63–71.

Townsend, B. K., & Ignash, J. M. (2003). Community college roles in teacher education: Current approaches and future possibilities. In B. K. Townsend & J. M. Ignash (Eds.), *The role of the community college in teacher education. New Directions for Community Colleges*, No. 121. San Francisco: Jossey-Bass, 5–16.

Walker, K. P. (2001). Opening the door to the baccalaureate degree. *Community College Review, 29*(2), 18–27.

Ward, C. V. L. (2001). A lesson from the British polytechnics for American community colleges. *Community College Review, 29*(2), 151–163.

Watson, C. (1971). *Innovation in higher education Canadian case study: New college system in Canada.* Toronto: Department of Education Planning, Ontario Institute for Studies in Education.

I I

A CAUTIONARY VIEW

Barbara K. Townsend

The community college baccalaureate (CCB) has become the lightning rod for opinions about the future of the U.S. community college and the nature of the baccalaureate degree. Those who support it contend that offering it is consistent with the community college mission to provide access to the underserved and to meet local community needs. Those who oppose it see it as potentially destroying the community college, either through damaging its focus on serving students undervalued by other institutions or through changing the institution to a four-year college, as has literally happened with community colleges in states regionally accredited by the Southern Association of Colleges and Schools (SACS). Still others oppose it on the grounds that the community college is not capable of offering a four-degree of the same quality as existing four-year institutions.

In this chapter, I explore two sets of opinions, both for and against; indicate necessary research and certain policy issues; and offer my own perspective about the CCB's impact on the community college and higher education in general.

However, I first clarify my definition of the CCB. By it, I mean simply and only a bachelor's degree awarded by a community college. I do not mean a bachelor's degree awarded by a four-year college or by a university in partnership with a community college. It is common practice for four-year institutions to partner with community colleges to provide at the two-year college the last two years of a baccalaureate. The four-year institution awards the degree, not the community college (Cook, 2000). Some community colleges with this arrangement bill themselves as offering the bachelor's degree—for example, Georgia's Snead State Community College, which has partnered with Athens State University (Snead State Community College, 2003), but a closer reading reveals that the community college does not award the baccalaureate.

The first two-year college to offer a baccalaureate degree was New York State's Fashion Institute of Technology in the 1970s (Fashion Institute of Technology, n.d.). Since that time so many community colleges have started offering baccalaureates that the most recent Carnegie Classification of [United States] Institutions of Higher Education (Carnegie Foundation, 2000) created a new category called baccalaureate/associate's colleges. These are institutions that primarily award associate's degrees and certificates, but at least 10 percent of their conferrals are bachelor's degrees. As of 2000, 57 institutions, most in the continental United States, received that designation, including public, private nonprofit, and private for-profit institutions (Carnegie Foundation, 2000). Of the 14 public ones in the continental United States, states' Web sites categorize almost half as two-year or community colleges. For example, Ohio's four are two-year public-university branch campuses of Ohio State University.

Positive Perspectives

Those who advocate the CCB argue that offering the degree is a logical extension of community colleges providing access to higher education and meeting local needs (Garmon, 1998; Walker, 2001). The community college is simply expanding its mission rather than changing it. This section looks at how proponents see the CCB affecting the community college in terms of access, meeting local needs, and mission.

Extending Educational Access

Proponents believe that community colleges offering the baccalaureate are extending access on two levels: offering the baccalaureate to people unable or unwilling to attend four-year institutions and providing credentials that most four-year institutions are unwilling to offer. In the words of Burke and Garmon (1995), typical candidates are people who "can't complete a bachelor's degree because they can't relocate, they're on limited incomes, they're held back by the transfer restrictions of receiving institutions, or they aren't equipped to face the hardships of readjusting to a new higher education environment" (p. 35). Some proponents see the CCB as a special kind of degree—in effect, the applied baccalaureate in certain career and technical education areas, such as manufacturing technology. The applied baccalaureate's "primary strength . . . would be its promise to provide specialized career-focused education that could train specialists for a new age of 'knowledge workers'" (Burke & Garmon, 1995). It would build on the foundation of an associate degree in science or an applied associate's in science. "The majority of technical and discipline major courses [would be] in the lower division [the associate degree program] and [there would be] a shift of some, but not all, general education to the upper division" (Wallace, 1999, p. 22). The CCB as an applied degree would differ from the traditional baccalaureate offered in the four-year sector. Also, because of most four-year colleges' reluctance to offer an applied baccalaureate, the community college would not be competing with senior institutions or duplicating their programs.

Making the baccalaureate available to groups that would not otherwise attain it is a way of democratizing the degree and evokes the founding mission of the land-grant universities, which made higher education available to many students and brought agriculture and the mechanic arts into the college curriculum (Rudolph, 1977).

Meeting Local Needs

The CCB not only democratizes higher education but may help meet local and state needs for employees in specific areas (Walker, 2001; Wallace, 1999). Efforts in Florida to authorize community colleges to provide the baccalaureate succeeded partly because they presented the credential as a "workforce baccalaureate" or "workforce bachelor's degree" (Florida State Board of Community Colleges, 1999) that would promote "local and statewide economic development" (p. 34). Under similar terms, community colleges in some states have received authority to offer the CCB in fields usually associated with four-year colleges, such as business administration and education. Also, Louisiana State University at Alexandria has received authorization to offer the bachelor of general studies and the bachelor of liberal studies (LSU Alexandria, n.d.).

Effect on Community College Mission

CCB proponents also claim that the degree will not affect the institutions' "core values of easy access, learner-centeredness, affordability, and convenience" (Walker, 2001, p. 26) or its "innate principles . . . [of] open-door admissions, low cost, developmental studies, local control, workforce development, continuing education, and the granting of associate degrees" (p. 26). In other words, CCB-granting institutions will still be truly community colleges, even if the Carnegie Foundation labels them baccalaureate/associate's colleges and regional accrediting associations see them as four-year institutions.

Negative Perspectives

While a Carnegie classification would seem to validate community colleges offering the baccalaureate, a number of concerns have surfaced about effects on mission, the quality of the CCB, and the future of the community college.

Effect on Mission

Will offering the baccalaureate prompt institutional leaders to neglect transfer and remedial education (Cook, 2000; Manzo, 2001; Pedersen, 2001)? One concern is that leaders may divert resources from traditional missions to the CCB (Cook, 2000). For example, Florida is funding the CCB in its four authorized institutions. However, more stringent fiscal times may end this assistance. Where will money come from to support costly CCB programs (Clark, 2002)? Also, the Southern Association of Colleges and Schools requires that CCB institutions meet four-year college standards: greater investments in library resources and student services (Pedersen, 2001). Professional accrediting associations will also affect allocations; for example, the National Council for Accreditation of Teacher Education (NCATE) insists on a low student–teacher ratio (Townsend & Ignash, 2003). Some fear that the money needed for these accreditation requirements may come from raising tuition fees for associate, diploma, and certificate programs (Pedersen, 2001).

Even if leaders advocating the CCB do not intend their colleges to change from open-access institutions welcoming nontraditional students, this may happen (Manzo, 2001). Faculty members hired to teach upper-division courses may well have different values from current instructors. These newcomers may not be happy in institutions that do not value faculty research. They may also be less supportive of open doors. They will also teach one or two fewer courses per semester than lower-division colleagues, since professional accrediting associations such as the NCATE and the National League for Nursing Accreditation Commission allow members to teach no more than 12 hours a semester or quarter. If upper-division instructors have a lighter teaching load, the resulting two-tiered faculty may profoundly affect the institutional culture. Additionally, when a community college replaces the president under whom it developed a CCB, it may tend to hire a successor from a four-year institution or someone who does not understand the college's traditional missions (Pedersen, 2001).

Quality of the Degree

Concern about the quality of the CCB has two dimensions. One is very general: The community college may not be able to offer a baccalaureate because it has never done so, was not designed to do so, and could not possibly do as well as four-year institutions. Critics maintain that four-year colleges are well-versed in the matter and thus there is no need for community colleges to do so. In Florida, the legislature authorized several million dollars to go to community colleges offering the CCB. Some observers think that these funds might be better spent by improving existing four-year programs rather than supporting mission creep.

More pointedly, some argue that the CCB is really an inferior degree that the market will not respect and that universities will not accept for admission to advanced degrees (Manzo, 2001; McKee, 2001; Wattenbarger, 2000). Additionally, they suggest that the CCB will not provide the same intellectual rigor as a baccalaureate from existing four-year colleges (Elliott, 2002).

Future of the Community College

Some commentators worry that the CCB will be the deathblow to the community college. As one colleague said with regard to the number of states that have authorized this degree, "We may really be at the end of the community college movement."

Certainly in those states with the CCB, most two-year schools offering them have become four-year institutions. Utah Valley Community College received authority in 1992. After changing its name to Utah Valley State College in 1994, it now is a four-year institution offering numerous baccalaureate programs (Utah Valley State College, n.d.). Utah's Dixie College became Dixie State College of Utah in 2000, when the Utah Board of Regents allowed it to change its mission. Its Web site calls it "a publicly supported state college with two interdependent tiers, function[ing] as a comprehensive community college while offering a limited number of quality baccalaureate programs" (Dixie State College of Utah, 2002, p. 1). Granted CCB status in 1997, Westark College in Arkansas became the four-year University of Arkansas at Fort Smith as of January 1, 2001 (University of Arkansas at Fort Smith, n.d.). By early 2003, two Florida community colleges had received CCB authorization and, by that fact, became four-year colleges, as their regional accrediting association mandated (Evelyn, 2003). Since their names must also reflect their four-year status, St. Petersburg Junior College became St. Petersburg College in 2001 (Evelyn, 2003), and Miami-Dade Community College became Miami-Dade College in 2003. Later in 2003, two other community colleges received CCB authorization.

Hawaii and Texas have also begun plans in which community colleges will offer bachelor's degrees. In May 2003, the University of Hawaii announced, as part of a reorganization plan, that three of its community colleges (Honolulu, Kapi'olani, and Maui) would offer baccalaureates. Although all seven of its community colleges must delete "community" from their institutional names, the three offering bachelor's degrees will in fact remain community colleges (Patton, 2003). In July 2003, on the basis of legislative authorization, the Texas Higher Education Coordinating Board allowed three community colleges (Brazoport College, Midland College, and South Texas Community College) to offer the baccalaureate in applied science and technology (*Community College Times*, 2003). Since the SACS accredits higher-education institutions in Texas, these three institutions will automatically become four-year schools, at least according to the definition of their regional accrediting association.

Issues for Policy and Research

Research

Proponents of the CCB who ask its critics, "Where's the beef?" will hear the fears described in this chapter. Critics might well ask supporters, "Where's the proof?" Where is proof that community colleges offering baccalaureates will not lose their founding commitment to open access and programs of less than four years? Where is proof that their baccalaureate is of high quality and acceptable in the market and as the basis for graduate study? Where is proof that two-year colleges will not disappear or at least lose stature because some of them do not want, or are not permitted, to offer the baccalaureate?

Only research conducted at the institutional, state, and national levels can answer these questions. Unfortunately, there has been little research conducted about the development of the CCB and its effects on community colleges and other higher-education institutions. McKee (2001) studied the development of the Bachelor of Manufacturing Technology at Westark College, now University of Arkansas at Fort Smith, and reported some of his research in Chapter 8 of this book. Officials at Westark told students that the degree might not be acceptable outside the local market or toward graduate studies. At the time McKee conducted his study, there was limited evidence about marketability and none about acceptance for graduate studies. Most writing about the CCB simply supports the degree or criticizes it.

The following kinds of research are necessary:

- Community colleges offering the baccalaureate need to monitor its effect on institutional culture, finances, and students, including students in certificate and diploma programs. Also, they should share their results with other community colleges and the broader educational community.

- CCB community colleges should research the CCB's effect on transfer rates when students remain rather than transferring to the four-year sector. This research is crucial in traditional four-year fields, such as business administration and education.

- States that legislate the CCB should monitor its impact on four-year colleges. Do their transfer enrollments drop substantially in baccalaureate areas offered by community colleges? Do some four-year institutions decide to offer four-year degrees at community colleges as a means to divert development of the CCB? Do some begin to lobby for offering more master's and doctoral degrees as a way of distinguishing themselves from the new baccalaureate/associate's colleges?

- States should examine not only whether more students attain the baccalaureate, but also whether the income and future educational attainment of CCB holders differ from those of people who earned a comparable baccalaureate at traditional four-year colleges.

At the national level, researchers and policy makers should study this phenomenon to see what factors facilitate or inhibit the development of the CCB as a degree option in public community colleges. They should also investigate the possible impact on national figures for baccalaureate completions. This research needs scrutiny by policy makers, both in states with the CCB and in states contemplating it.

Policy Issues

Policy issues to be considered include the following:

- Before authorization of any CCBs, should four-year institutions have the right to decide if they are willing to offer the degree desired by the community college—for example, a Bachelor of Applied Science in Manufacturing Technology—either at the four-year site or on-site at the community college? This approach is the one followed in Florida.

- Similarly, should partnerships between two- and four-year colleges for purposes of offering bachelor's degrees preempt community colleges' requests to offer a CCB? For instance in 2003, Florida denied two community colleges authority to offer a CCB because the State Board of Education recommended instead a partnership with local four-year schools (Florida Department of Education, 2003).

- For institutions with the CCB, should there be a limit on the percentage of conferrals that could be CCBs each year? States that adopt this approach might define community colleges as institutions whose baccalaureate conferrals are no more than 20 percent each year. Doing so might be one way to preserve community colleges as an institutional type.

- Should community colleges offer the baccalaureate only in truly applied fields and not in fields traditionally associated with four-year college education, such as education and liberal studies. When offering the baccalaureate in traditional fields, the community college is moving beyond a special baccalaureate niche of applied degrees in fields such as automotive or manufacturing technology and into the educational territory of four-year institutions.

- Can transfer rates continue as a performance measure for community colleges offering the CCB in such fields as education and nursing?

- Will the offering of applied baccalaureates in career and technical areas affect federal legislation about career and technical education, especially since these programs have historically taken less time to complete than traditional baccalaureates?

The Future

The emergence of the applied baccalaureate may be revitalizing discussions of what constitutes a bachelor's degree. Is the baccalaureate four years of progressively more difficult study, with the first two years of general education providing the skills and intellectual development necessary for advanced, upper-division work? Alternatively, is it simply or primarily a collection of lower-division courses that reach the number required for a baccalaureate, normally 120 credit hours or more? The development of the upside-down applied baccalaureate, which concentrates general education in the last two years and the bulk of the major in first- and second-year technical courses (Cook, 2000; Townsend, 2001), reflects the latter view. The major or technical field of study does not build on general education. However, several four-year colleges have supported and developed the upside-down degree, independent of any effort by community colleges. Perhaps the controversy over the CCB will force a "reconceptualization of the baccalaureate" (McKee, 2001, p. 91), which appears to be the stance taken by the North Central accrediting association (Higher Education Learning Commission, 2001).

Emergence of the CCB may inspire more four-year colleges to offer applied baccalaureates (McKee, 2001). Doing so allowed Arizona's four-year institutions to prevent the state's community colleges from offering the baccalaureate. In 1998, Arizona State University–East became the first four-year institution to offer the applied baccalaureate, or bachelor of applied science (Arizona Board of Regents, n.d.). The threat of the CCB may also motivate more four-year colleges to offer bachelor's degrees at two-year colleges by providing the last two years of the degree. However, even though Westark College had a university center on campus, its president still pursued the CCB (McKee, 2001), calling it an "expansion" of this approach.

What is clear is that, because of the CCB, more two-year college students will have access to the baccalaureate. Perhaps partly to fend off the CCB, more four-year colleges will collaborate with community colleges to offer baccalaureate programs at the two-year sites, and some will develop applied baccalaureates that accept in transfer two-year college students' applied study. Also, apparently more community colleges will receive authority to offer the baccalaureate.

What is less clear is what will happen to the community college as an institutional type. Will it become like other educational institutions that served a purpose for a while and then morphed into other institutional types? For example, normal schools converted to teacher's colleges, which changed into state colleges, which reemerged as state universities. Nowadays, the United States has only five teacher's colleges (Carnegie Foundation, 2000). Similarly, women's colleges have almost disappeared; there were only five two-year women's colleges as of 2000 (Townsend, 2001). Only time will tell if the CCB is the catalyst for transforming the majority of community colleges into baccalaureate/associate's colleges, which might eventually become baccalaureate colleges-general, in which over half of the degrees conferred are baccalaureates.

References

Arizona Board of Regents. (n.d.). *Abstract: Progress report on Arizona public post-secondary education*. Retrieved on August 10, 2003, from www.abor.asu.edu/1_the_regents/reports_factbook/progress/abstract

Burke, T. R., & Garmon, J. F. (1995). The community college baccalaureate. *Community College Journal, 65*(7), 35–38.

Carnegie Foundation for the Advancement of Teaching. (2000). *Carnegie classification of institutions of higher education.* Retrieved August 8, 2003, from www.carnegiefoundation.org/Classification/CIE2000/defNotes/Definitions.htm

Clark, L. (2002). MDCC allowed to offer 4-year degree. *Miami Herald.*

Community College Times. (2003). Three Texas community colleges to offer bachelors, 5.

Cook, A. (2000). *Community college baccalaureate degrees: A delivery model for the future?* Denver, CO: Education Commission of the States.

Dixie State College of Utah. (2002). General information. Retrieved August 8, 2003, from www.dixie.edu/gen/vision.html

Elliott, M. (2002). Decision on Edison four-year degrees put off until March. *Naples Daily News.*

Evelyn, J. (2003). Making waves in Miami. *Chronicle of Higher Education,* A34–35.

Fashion Institute of Technology. (n.d.). *History/Mission.* Retrieved August 8, 2003, from www.fitnyc.suny.edu/aspx/Content.aspx?menu=Past:aboutFit:HistoryMission

Florida Department of Education. (2003). *Access to the baccalaureate: Community colleges offering four-year degrees.* Retrieved on May 23, 2003, from www.flboe.org/cc

Florida State Board of Community Colleges. (1999). *The Florida community college system: A strategic plan for the millennium 1998–2003.* Retrieved August 19, 2003, from www.dcc.firn.edu/Vision/strategic_plan.pdf

Garmon, J. (1998). The baccalaureate revisited. *Community College Week,* 4–5.

Higher Education Learning Commission. (2001). *Baccalaureate education in the community college setting.* Retrieved on May 23, 2003, from www.ncahigherlearningcommission.org/resources/bacc_ed_cc/

LSU Alexandria. (n.d.). *Four-year LSUA update.* Retrieved on December 8, 2003, from www.lsua.edu/community/4year.htm

Manzo, K. K. (2001). Community colleges: Breaking through to the other side. *Community College Week,* 6–8.

McKee, J. V. (2001). *Factors and issues surrounding development of one community college baccalaureate degree program.* Ed.D. Dissertation from Oregon State University.

Patton, M. (2003). University of Hawaii reorganizes community colleges. *Community College Times,* 10.

Pedersen, R. P. (2001). You say you want an evolution? Read the fine print first. *Community College Week,* 4–5.

Rudolph, F. (1977). *Curriculum: A history of the American undergraduate course of study since 1636.* San Francisco: Jossey-Bass.

Snead State Community College. (2003). *Snead state community college partners with ASU.* Retrieved on August 8, 2003, from www.snead.edu/news/asu-announcement.htm

Townsend, B. K. (2001). *The shrinking divide between upper and lower division courses: A baccalaureate meltdown?* Invited speech at the Phil Hardin Leadership Symposium, Annual Mississippi Association of Colleges and Universities, Gulf Port, MS.

Townsend, B. K., & Ignash, J. (Eds.) (2003). *The role of the community college in teacher education. New Directions for Community Colleges,* No. 121. San Francisco: Jossey-Bass.

University of Arkansas at Fort Smith. (n.d.). *UA Fort Smith history.* Retrieved on August 12, 2003, from www.uafortsmith.edu/About/UAFFortSmithHistory?sin=

Utah Valley State College. (n.d.). *Degrees—Listed by type.* Retrieved on August 10, 2003, from www.uvsc.edu/catalog/degree/degres.html

Walker, K. P. (2001). Opening the door to the baccalaureate degree. *Community College Review, 29*(2), 18–28.

Wallace, S. R. (1999). Meeting the needs of information-age employers. *Community College Journal, 69*(6), 21–22.

Wattenbarger, J. (2000). Colleges should stick to what they do best. *Community College Week, 13*(18), 4–5.

12

THE COMMUNITY COLLEGE BACCALAUREATE

TOWARD AN AGENDA FOR POLICY AND RESEARCH

Michael L. Skolnik and Deborah L. Floyd

The foregoing chapters have related the history of the community college baccalaureate, described existing models, and attempted to clarify the distinction between the community college baccalaureate in which the community college offers a complete baccalaureate on its own and other baccalaureate models. As is to be expected among authors, some of whom have themselves been pioneers and early adopters of this somewhat controversial innovation in the community college, earlier chapters have included some passionate advocacy for the community college baccalaureate as an important next step in the evolution of the community college. At the same time, we have tried to make readers aware that there are criticisms of this movement and legitimate reasons for concern about how the community college could be affected negatively in the process of incorporating this new function.

Most of the foregoing chapters conclude with a list of questions or issues for policy and research. The purpose of this chapter is not repeat all those questions or combine them into a giant master list, but to identify the most important common themes among these issues, and to offer some concluding comments that may help to place the material presented in the earlier chapters in a broader policy and research context.

Among the possible frameworks for viewing the community college baccalaureate is one that focuses on the characteristics of the programs themselves and another that focuses on the implications of these programs for institutions and the structure of entire systems of postsecondary education.

With respect to the first of these, the programs themselves; as the earlier chapters show, there are two principal rationales for, or goals of, the community college baccalaureate. One is to *increase access to the baccalaureate degree* in general for people whose opportunity is limited within existing arrangements for postsecondary education by such factors as geographic location, finances, and learning styles. The clientele affected would include particularly, but not only, nontraditional students. Increasing access to the baccalaureate degree can be justified both on grounds of equity and for the contributions to the economy and society that further education will enable these individuals to make.

The other rationale for the community college baccalaureate is to *provide a different type of baccalaureate education* than is typically provided by universities; one that combines a more hands-on type of learning with academic study, producing graduates that some observers believe will be in high demand by industry. This type of baccalaureate degree has been called a workforce baccalaureate, or an applied baccalaureate degree, though the precise ways in which it is actually differentiated from a conventional, or academic, baccalaureate degree have been difficult to explicate precisely.

Although these two rationales for the community college baccalaureate can be distinguished from one another conceptually, in practice they may often coincide. Such would be the case when, for example, the thing that holds someone back who has completed two years of study in an occupational program in a community college is not the absence of an accessible university in the community, but the fact that this university does not offer a baccalaureate with a similar applied occupational focus as the community college program, or in an area of study that is directly related to what the student did in the two years of study at the community college.

As Thomas E. Furlong pointed out in Chapter 7, many of the areas in which consideration is being given to developing new baccalaureate programs are technical fields where the community college offers an associate degree but there is no corresponding baccalaureate program offered by a university, at least within the same region or state (e.g., dental hygiene or orthotics). Programs of an applied nature that build upon a community college's two-year workforce-oriented programs would appear to comprise the majority of community college baccalaureate programs thus far. This is particularly the case in the Canadian provinces of Alberta and Ontario where the colleges have been authorized to offer applied baccalaureate degree programs—and only applied degree programs. This type of program has been common among the early community college baccalaureate programs in the United States too, though perhaps of a lower priority than programs in teacher education—as was the case at both St. Petersburg College and Great Basin College. Given the numerical significance of the applied type of baccalaureate programs thus far, it would seem that high on the research agenda should be curriculum analysis aimed at explicating the characteristics of this class of programs and how they differ from more traditional baccalaureates.

Another way of gaining perspective on the community college baccalaureate is to look at its implications for the way that institutions are viewed within postsecondary education systems. A predominant feature of the way that we view postsecondary institutions is associated with the practice of classifying them as either two-year or four-year institutions, or in the terminology used in Canada, as either community colleges or universities. Along with this categorization come expectations, and often legislative or policy stipulations, regarding institutional missions and allowable activities.

Institutions that wish to generally maintain the mission of a community college while offering a limited number of baccalaureate programs don't fit comfortably within this classification framework or the set of expectations about institutional activity that is associated with the framework. Perhaps regional accrediting associations, the Carnegie classification system and organizations such as the American Association of Community Colleges need a new classification scheme that recognizes these "new" colleges, as suggested by Deborah L. Floyd in Chapter 3. In Canada, as noted by Michael L. Skolnik in Chapter 4, the national statistics agency in Canada has proposed the creation of a new hybrid community college-university category to capture this new reality.

Some Key Policy and Research Questions

In the remainder of this chapter, we identify some of the key policy questions that were identified in the earlier chapters and comment on the associated challenges for research.

At the broadest level of generality, there are two major policy questions concerning the community college baccalaureate: should community colleges embark on this road, and if so, how should they do it? An important subquestion under the second question—that perhaps warrants being elevated to the status of a third major question—is how can institutions implement the community college baccalaureate without undermining important community college values and commitments regarding accessibility, serving the most disadvantaged learners, and student-centeredness?

Perhaps it is too early in the experience of those community colleges that have implemented the community college baccalaureate for drawing conclusions about how well they have maintained their commitment to traditional community-college values, and if so, how they managed to do this. Still, it would seem important to initiate research on this issue in the case of the institutions that have been involved in the community college baccalaureate the longest; for example, those in Alberta that commenced offering applied baccalaureate programs in 1996. Particularly valuable would be case study research that documents the broad impacts that implementing the baccalaureate has had throughout the institution, including on its culture; the nature and strength of efforts made simultaneously to maintain or strengthen the institution's commitment to traditional community-college values; and how and how well the various clients of the institution continue to be served.

So far as the first major policy question is concerned, whether or not to take the first steps in the direction of the community college baccalaureate, colleges and system officials in each jurisdiction should first do needs assessments in which they attempt to measure the unmet need for the baccalaureate from students and employers and assess the barriers that prevent higher baccalaureate completion rates. They should also examine the capabilities of local four-year institutions in the field of any proposed program and explore the potential for collaboration with those other institutions, along the lines of the approach suggested in Chapter 7 by Thomas E. Furlong, and employing models such as those described by Albert L. Lorenzo in Chapter 5.

Both the community colleges in each state and state-level education authorities should be party to the decisions about whether the community colleges in the state should get into baccalaureate degree provision, and if so, how to do it. Probably in all cases, community colleges will need some type of state-level authorization to offer baccalaureate degree programs, and even where state officials are persuaded of the value of this innovation, they will need the (enthusiastic) support and capacity of local community colleges for implementation.

Dialogue between local and state levels is important, though the forms of that dialogue will vary considerably depending upon the governance structure for postsecondary education in the state or province. It is also important to involve the universities in this dialogue, as the community college baccalaureate has significant implications for the universities, and the overarching goal of public policy should be to achieve the *combined* use of the resources of the universities and community colleges in each state and province that will bring the greatest benefit to students.

In some cases, the primary impetus for the community college baccalaureate may come from leaders of particular colleges, reflecting expressions of demand from their communities; anchored in dialogue between the college, local employers, and other community groups; and supported by local needs-assessment studies. In other cases, state officials may be ahead of the curve, armed with data from their own research studies. In either case, dialogue between levels is essential—both in arriving at a go/no-go decision and in designing the process, criteria, and conditions for the implementation of the community college baccalaureate.

Policy making related to the community college baccalaureate will require good state or provincial and national data. At minimum, there should be data that identifies all community college baccalaureate and related programs—in terms of the categorization given in Chapter 3 by Deborah L. Floyd—and provides information on basic program characteristics. Such basic data could provide a starting point that would assist in designing more analytical studies on student outcomes and program effectiveness of the type suggested in Chapter 11 by Barbara K. Townsend. With respect to the basic data needs, it is not at all clear where the resources or leadership should come from. Several parties have an obvious interest in monitoring the development of the community college baccalaureate (e.g. the American Association of Community Colleges, the Community College Baccalaureate Association, government educational and statistical agencies, and various agencies concerned with trends and developments in postsecondary education). There is some question, however, how mandates, interest, and resources come together.

Two additional policy-related themes which recur throughout this book are those pertaining to funding and to the quality and value of the degrees. Regarding the first of these issues, the points that have been made are several and possibly contradictory. On the one hand, some observers have maintained that one of the attractive features of the community college baccalaureate program (especially to governments) is its more economical method of expanding baccalaureate enrollment than that of four-year institutions. However, the research to confirm this assumption is absent, and other observers have identified inadequate funding as a major problem for institutions that are offering community college baccalaureate programs. For example, in Chapter 10, Berta Vigil Laden reports that, in her study of Ontario colleges, inadequate funding emerged as the most important policy issue. Funding and finance would seem to be an important area for research; for example, comparing the costs of baccalaureate programs in two-year and four-year institutions.

As noted earlier, a predominant characteristic of community college baccalaureate programs is their intent to prepare people for the workforce, often in rather narrowly defined job fields. Yet, the jury is still out on how employers will regard these new degrees. It is quite possible that employers who already have high regard for the associate's degree graduates they have hired out of community colleges will have the same opinion of the graduates of the community college's baccalaureate programs. On the other hand, the idea of community colleges offering baccalaureate degrees is relatively new and novel, and it is thus important that research be undertaken to document and analyze the workforce experience of graduates of these programs.

Likely, the perceived value of the degrees will bear a connection to their perceived quality. Achieving accreditation, including specialized program accreditation where applicable, will be one important indicator of the quality of these new programs. Adopting academic standards that are comparable to those of four-year institutions also could add to the credibility of the community college baccalaureate programs. However, a potential downside of modeling their program requirements too closely on those of the universities is that often the community college baccalaureate programs are intended to provide a different type of educational experience than the university. This potential conflict of goals — attempting to offer a new type of baccalaureate program, but at the same time, having the program accepted by the educational establishment—is likely to be particularly apparent with regard to questions of transfer to other postsecondary institutions or when graduates of these programs apply to master's programs.

In the various forums that we have attended where the community college baccalaureate was being discussed, we have been struck by the amount of international interest there is in this topic. The bringing together of contributors from both the United States and Canada in this project is a reflection of how interest in this topic extends across borders, but that interest extends well beyond the North American continent. In speculating about the reason for such interest, we would observe that in almost every nation, postsecondary education systems consist of both universities that are quite similar to their counterparts in North America, and a variety of other types of postsecondary institutions, whose missions restrict them from offering baccalaureate programs. Yet in other countries, as in North America, there seems to be a perception that there is a greater demand for the baccalaureate than the universities can, or are willing, to meet.

Also, among educators in "second sector" institutions, there is a common perception that the baccalaureate is an appropriate credential to recognize graduation from an applied program of the highest level of sophistication that the institution can offer. Insofar as such perceptions are widely shared in other countries, it is understandable that educators from those other countries would look with great interest upon the emergence of baccalaureate programs in the non-university sector in the United States and Canada.

In other countries, as in Canada and the United States, community colleges and other non-university institutions may not wish to offer many baccalaureate programs but having the recognition to offer just a few of those programs can enhance the academic credibility and stature of the institution to the benefit of all its programs and activities.

Community colleges have a proud egalitarian tradition of collaborating and leading efforts to pave the path for access to postsecondary education for millions of people in many countries. This movement of community colleges in leading efforts to expand baccalaureate opportunities is likely to gain even more momentum as this unique sector of postsecondary education truly embraces the challenges of opportunity, and does so for the right reason—students.

13

THE COMMUNITY COLLEGE BACCALAUREATE

RESOURCES AND INFORMATION

Michelle Eastham[1]

The community college baccalaureate is an emerging trend in the United States, that has been gaining momentum over the past decade. Although relatively new to the United States, the community college baccalaureate is not a new phenomenon in Canada and Britain. Because offering bachelor's degrees at community colleges is a fairly recent event, a substantial body of research has not yet been created on the subject. Most of the literature can be found on Web sites, in newspapers, and in journal articles.

This chapter presents a compilation of U.S. and Canadian resources, including Web sites, articles or papers, and books or chapters. The materials reviewed reflect current views on the subject and should give readers the tools to locate additional resources. The citations offer both support and criticism of the baccalaureate.

[1] The contributions and suggestions of Michael L. Skolnik, Deborah L. Floyd, and Kenneth P. Walker were extremely helpful with the development of this chapter. The author wishes to acknowledge their collaborative support with compiling these sources.

United States

Web Sites

American Association of Community Colleges (AACC): www.aacc. nche.edu/
The AACC's Web site features academic resources, a community college finder, research, and publications for higher education administrators and students worldwide.

Contact Information:
American Association of Community Colleges (AACC)
One Dupont Circle NW, Suite 410
Washington, DC 20036
Phone: 202.728.0200
Fax: 202.833.2467
www.aacc.nche.edu/

Community College Baccalaureate Association (CCBA): www.accbd.org/
The purpose of the CCBA is: "To promote better access to the baccalaureate degree on community college campuses, and to serve as a resource for information on various models for accomplishing this purpose" (CCBA Web site). The association makes current information and legislation regarding the community college baccalaureate accessible to the public. Specifically, the Web site provides information regarding the CCBA's annual conference, access to a number of full text articles dealing with the degree, and full text access to its newsletter, the *Beacon*. Through 2003, there have been eight issues of the *Beacon* published.
Sample resources from the CCBA Web site:

Floyd, D. L. (November 15, 2003). *The community college baccalaureate: An emerging trend*. Paper presented at the Association for the Study of Higher Education, Portland, OR.

Abstract: Floyd defines the community college baccalaureate and offers a typology of four models: articulation, certification, university center, and the community college baccalaureate. Key characteristics of the last model and preliminary findings from a survey conducted by the CCBA are given.

Walker, K. P. (April 2001). An open door to the bachelor's degree. *Leadership Abstracts, 4*(2).

Abstract: Walker has conducted single-institution research and focus groups; results show that many place-bound community college students are interested in earning bachelor's degrees. The author discusses the need for change in American higher education and offers the community college baccalaureate as a solution. Seven benefits of offering bachelor's degrees at community colleges are given.

Walker, K. P. (July–August 2000). Reinventing the community college. *On the Horizon, 8*(4).

Abstract: The future of the community college is discussed. The author asks, "What will it be and how will it get there?" and answers, "One thing is certain—the community college of the future will not be the community college of the past." Walker discusses the importance of expanding the community college mission to include bachelor's degrees while retaining open-door admissions. The growing movement towards the community college baccalaureate degree is presented.

Walker, K. P. (March 2000). Community college baccalaureate degree. *Trustee Quarterly,* pp. 13–16.

Abstract: The author asserts that the community college baccalaureate is a rapidly emerging issue in American higher education. He presents evidence that the baccalaureate is a way to meet the ever-increasing demand for degree access at an affordable cost. The benefits of offering bachelor's degrees at community colleges are presented.

Walker, K. P. (Fall 1999). Workforce bachelor's degree. *Presidency, 2*(3), pp. 27–30.

Abstract: The author cites a report by the Commission on National Investment in Higher Education, which claims that there is "a time bomb ticking under the nation's social and economic foundations. . . . the opportunity to go to college will be denied to millions of Americans unless sweeping changes are made." Walker asserts that the national crisis in higher education calls for creative solutions and offers the community college baccalaureate as one such solution.

Contact Information:
Community College Baccalaureate Association
P.O. Box 60210
Ft. Myers, FL 33906
Phone: 239.947.8085
Fax: 239.489.9250
www.accbd.org/

ERIC Clearinghouse: www.eric.ed.gov/
Educational Resource Information Center (ERIC) is supported by the U.S. Department of Education and contains over one million documents and journal articles on education-related topics. Full text articles are available through ERIC Document Reproduction Services (EDRS). Sample resources:

Cook, A. (2002). *Community college baccalaureate degrees: A delivery model for the future? A policy paper.* (ERIC No. ED439765).

Abstract: This paper discusses the community college baccalaureate. It proposes that changing demographics, fiscal concerns, and community expectations are creating pressure to add the granting of four-year degrees to the traditional mission of the community college. The author presents arguments for the community college baccalaureate as well as concerns from scholars and policy makers.

Levin J. (2002). *Institutional identity: The community college as a baccalaureate degree granting institution.* (ERIC No. ED474578).

Abstract: This paper focuses on community colleges as baccalaureate-granting institutions. The discussion is based on research projects undertaken in both the United States and Canada that explore offering bachelor's degrees at two-year institutions. Results show that the institutional identity of the community college has been altered as a result.

Mills, K. (2003). *Community college baccalaureates: Some critics decry the trend as "Mission Creep."* (ERIC No. ED473685).

Abstract: St. Petersburg College (SPC) in Florida is a community college that has added three bachelor's degrees: education, technology management, and nursing. This author presents the critics' arguments against community college baccalaureates, suggesting that they are inferior and that offering them will change the school's mission. However, supporters argue that the colleges are meeting a community need that has not been adequately met by four-year institutions.

Contact Information:
ERIC Clearinghouse
2277 Research Boulevard, 6M
Rockville, MD 20850
Toll Free: 800.LET.ERIC (538.3742)
Phone: 301.519.5157
Fax: 301.519.6760
E-mail: accesseric@accesseric.org
www.eric.ed.gov/

The Higher Learning Commission: www.ncahigherlearningcommission.org/

The commission is part of the North Central Association of Colleges and Schools. The association was founded in 1895 as a membership organization for educational institutions. It is committed to developing and maintaining high standards of excellence in higher education. Sample resource:

Task force executive summary with recommendations. (February 23, 2001). Task Force Meeting Report. The Higher Learning Commission North Central Association of Colleges and Schools. Available at: www .ncahigherlearningcommission.org/resources/bacc_ed_cc/index.html

Abstract: In August 1998, the executive director of the Higher Learning Commission presented to the Board of Trustees the first institutional request from a community college to have its accreditation extended to a small number of programs leading to a bachelor of applied technology. Because of the precedent-setting nature of this request, the board decided to follow a unique course of action. This document reports the actions taken by the task force.

Contact Information
Higher Learning Commission
30 N. LaSalle Street, Suite 2400
Chicago, IL 60602-2504
Phone: 800.621.7440 or 312.263.0456
Fax: 312.263.7462
www.ncahigherlearningcommission.org/

UMI ProQuest Digital Dissertations: wwwlib.umi.com/dissertations/
This database contains over two million doctoral dissertations and master's theses. The database includes bibliographical citations for materials ranging from the first U.S. dissertation, accepted in 1861, to those accepted as recently as last semester. You can order any dissertation online, and it is delivered to your home within four to five working days. This process will cost about $34. Two specific dissertations that may be of interest include:

Burrows, B. (2002). *The vertical extension of Florida's community college system: A case study of politics and entrepreneurial leadership*. Dissertation, University of Texas–Austin.

Abstract: This dissertation explores the history of the community college mission. The author examines the community college baccalaureate in Florida, focusing on St. Petersburg College. The implications of adding bachelor's degrees to community colleges are discussed.

McKee, J. (2001). *Factors and issues surrounding development of one community college baccalaureate degree program*. Dissertation, Oregon State University.

Abstract: This thesis argues that the community college baccalaureate potentially represents the next major community college mission shift in the United States. The purpose of the author's research is to describe the factors and issues surrounding the development of the three-year bachelor of manufacturing technology degree program at Westark College in Arkansas.

Contact Information:
UMI ProQuest Digital Dissertations
Phone: 800.521.0600 ex. 2873 (to place an order)
E-mail: core_service@umi.com
Digital Dissertations: www.lib.umi.com/dissertations/

Journals and Periodicals

Chronicle of Higher Education: The *Chronicle of Higher Education* is
the number-one news source for college and university related information. The *Chronicle* is published weekly, and a subscription is required
to gain access. A subscription includes a weekly printed copy of the
Chronicle mailed to your home, access to all *Chronicle* articles online,
and a daily e-mail newsletter. Sample resource:

Evelyn, J. (April 11, 2003). Making waves in Miami: A leading community
college offers bachelor's degrees, reflecting national tension between 2 and
4 year sectors. *Chronicle of Higher Education,* pp. 34–35.

Abstract: The author describes the growing phenomenon of adding
bachelor's degrees to community colleges in Florida. The author presents some of the tensions between the two- and four-year colleges,
such as decreased enrollment at four-year institutions as a result of the
community college baccalaureate.

Contact Information:
The *Chronicle of Higher Education*
1255 23rd Street NW, Suite 700
Washington, DC 20037
Phone: 202.466.1000
www.chronicle.com/

Community College Journal: The *Community College Journal* is an
American Association of Community Colleges publication. It features
articles by experts on community colleges, a discussion of higher-
education issues, and profiles of leaders in the field. Each issue reviews
news and information from a national perspective and presents the most
up-to-date surveys, research, and practices. This journal is published six

times a year and is available only by subscription for $29. Sample resources:

Burke, T., & Garmon, J. (August–September 1995). The community college-baccalaureate. *Community College Journal, 65*(7), pp. 34–38.

Abstract: This article discusses the possibility of a community college baccalaureate and offers it as an alternative to the traditional bachelor's degree for students in occupational fields desiring further education. The authors indicate that the community college baccalaureate offers students a chance to complete their bachelor's degree in high-demand fields.

Walker, K. P., & Zeiss, P. A. (December 2000–January 2001). Designs for change: Degrees and skills. *Community College Journal, 71*(3), pp. 8–11.

Abstract: Because of workforce demands, community colleges are pressed to adapt the degree programs that they offer. Colleges in Arkansas, Hawaii, Nevada, New York, Pennsylvania, Oregon, Utah, and West Virginia, as well as in Canada, currently offer the baccalaureate. According to the authors, offering the bachelor's degree at community colleges has moral, social, economic, and political value.

Contact Information:
Community College Journal
Atwood Publishing
11600 College Boulevard
Overland Park, KS 66210
Phone: 913.469.1110 ext. 298
Fax: 913.469.0806
www.aacc.nche.edu/Content/NavigationMenu/ResourceCenter/
AACCPublications/CommunityCollegeJournal/CommunityCollege
Journal.htm

Community College Journal of Research and Practice (CCJRP): The *CCJRP* is a refereed journal and the only community college-related journal that is international in scope. It contains information for both researchers and practitioners in higher education and in the behavioral and social sciences. It aims to increase awareness of issues facing community colleges by providing a forum for the discussion of ideas, research, and empirically tested educational innovations. The journal is available by subscription only. A yearly subscription includes ten issues at a cost of $129, with a reduced price for members of the American Association of Community Colleges' Council for the Study of Community Colleges. Sample resources:

Floyd, D. L., & Walker, D. A. (September 2003). Community college teacher education: A typology, challenging issues, and state views. *Community College Journal of Research and Practice, 27*, pp. 643–663.

Abstract: This article analyzes and reports the findings of a 2002 survey of state directors of U.S. community colleges s regarding their perceptions of the current role of community colleges in teacher-education programming in their respective states. Four distinct models emerged among the states that have authorized community colleges to adopt or expand their role in teacher education: articulation, university center, certification, and community college baccalaureate. Only Nevada and Florida reported that the last-named model was currently being implemented, with other states such as Utah noting that community colleges that had been approved to confer baccalaureate degrees were now formally classified as four-year colleges. Floyd and Walker describe a number of ramifications relating to policy and future research.

Contact Information:
Community College Journal of Research and Practice
Taylor & Francis Publishers
325 Chestnut Street, Suite 800
Philadelphia, PA 19106
Phone: 800.354.1420
Fax: 215.625.8914
www.tandf.co.uk/journals/tf/10668926.html

Community College Review: The *Community College Review* is a refereed journal that has been published by the Department of Adult and Community College Education at the University of North Carolina since 1973. The purpose of this publication is to disseminate research that focuses on issues in community college education. This journal is published quarterly and available through a subscription priced at $65 per year. Some of the articles are available in full text online. Members of the Council for the Study of Community Colleges may receive a reduced price for subscriptions. Resources from this publication:

Walker, K. P. (Fall 2001). Opening the door to the baccalaureate degree. *Community College Review, 29*(2), pp. 18–28.

Abstract: This author discusses the college system in several Canadian provinces, which allows community colleges to grant bachelor's degrees, and makes a case for the U.S. community college baccalaureate. Walker claims that community colleges can offer bachelor's degrees at a lower cost to both students and taxpayers.

Ward, C. (Fall 2001). A lesson from the British polytechnics for American community colleges. *Community College Review, 29*(2), pp. 1–17.

Abstract: This article presents examples of British polytechnic institutions' conversion into universities and warns the United States to avoid transforming community colleges into baccalaureate-granting institutions. The author claims that adding the bachelor's degree to community colleges alters their original mission and places a burden on them to convert completely into four-year institutions.

Contact Information:
Community College Review
Department of Adult & Community College Education
College of Education and Psychology–NC State University
Box 7801
Raleigh, NC 27695
Phone: 919.515.6248
Fax: 919.515.4039
E-mail: ashley_byram@ncsu.edu
www.ced.ncsu.edu:8480/acce/ccr/

The Review of Higher Education: Published by the Association for the Study of Higher Education, The *Review of Higher Education* is a refereed journal that explores timely issues facing today's colleges and universities. The journal includes peer-reviewed articles, essays, reviews and research findings. Resource:

Levin, J. S. (in press). The challenge to identify: The community college as a baccalaureate degree granting institution. *The Review of Higher Education*. Johns Hopkins University Press.

Abstract: Drawing from globalization theory and institutional theory, the author explores the idea that the introduction of baccalaureate degree programming may lead to alteration of the community college's institutional identity. This article reports the findings of a multi-site, two nation investigation that examines potential outcomes of the baccalaureate granting status for community colleges and questions whether the institution can maintain its traditional role.

Contact Information:
The Review of Higher Education
Johns Hopkins University Press
2715 North Charles Street
Baltimore, MD 21218-4319
Phone: 410.516.6900
www.press.jhu.edu/journals/review_of_higher_education/

Community College Times: Sponsored by the American Association of Community Colleges, the *Community College Times* newspaper reports happenings at community colleges around the United States, including issues such as controversies, protests, tuition changes, grants, legislation, and people's moves. *Community College Times* gives higher-education scholars a closer look at the critical issues facing two-year colleges today. Sample resource:

Walker, K. P. (November 5, 1997). Should community colleges offer bachelor's degrees? *Community College Times, 9*(21).

Abstract: Walker argues that research continues to emphasize the need for dramatic changes in education at all levels and offers to make better use of the vast resources of community colleges as a solution. Individual and societal benefits of the community college baccalaureate are given.

Contact Information:
Community College Times
One Dupont Circle NW, Suite 410
Washington, DC 20036
Phone: 202.728.0200 ext. 206
Fax: 202.223.9390
www.aacc.nche.edu/Content/NavigationMenu/ResourceCenter/
AACCPublications/CommunityCollegeTimes/CommunityCollege
Times.htm

Community College Week: *Community College Week* is an independent source of in-depth information about two-year colleges and is published biweekly. A subscription is required to gain access to information published. Sample resource:

Garmon, J. (June 26, 2000). No need for war with four-year institutions. *Community College Week, 12*(35).

Abstract: This article discusses the ideology behind the community college mission and is examined in comparison to the four-year college mission. The author discusses the practical implications and political forces at play when community colleges offer workforce bachelor's degrees.

Troumpoucis, P. (2004). The best of both worlds? *Community College Week.* *16*(18).

Abstract: One of the major purposes of the community college baccalaureate is to improve access to four year degrees for non-traditional students. This article reports interviews with experts and leaders about the reasons for community colleges offering baccalaureate programs and concerns about how this new emphasis will alter the traditional mission of community colleges.

Contact Information:
Community College Week
10520 Warwick Avenue, Suite B-8
Fairfax, VA 22030-3136
Phone: 703.385.2981
Fax: 703.385.1839
www.ccweek.com/

New Directions for Community Colleges (NDCC): *NDCC* is a quarterly journal containing six to eight edited articles, including a sources and information chapter. Every issue has a central theme and is aimed at community college scholars and practitioners. Subscriptions are available through Jossey-Bass for $57 a year, or a single issue can be purchased for $25. Sample resource:

Bers, T., & Calhoun, H. (Eds.). (Spring, 2002). Next steps for the community college. *New Directions for Community Colleges,* No. 117.

Abstract: This particular issue—"Next Steps for the Community College"—provides an overview of contemporary literature and practice in areas of major concern to community colleges: transfer rates, vocational education, assessment of student learning, and much more. The authors review recent research on topics of importance, highlighting both consensus and contradictions, and identify critical challenges that community colleges face.

Townsend B. K. & Ignash, J. M. (Eds.). (Spring, 2003). The role of the community college in teacher education. *New Directions for Community Colleges*, No. 121.

Abstract: This describes the various roles community colleges as assuming in teacher education, including traditional ways of providing the first two years of an undergraduate degree and more controversial ways, such as baccalaureate degrees in teacher education and alternative certification programs.

Contact Information:
John Wiley & Sons, Inc.
Attn: Subscription Department
111 River Street
Hoboken, NJ 07030-5774
Phone: 201.748.6645 or 800.825.7550
Fax: 201.748.6021
E-mail: subinfo@wiley.com
www.josseybass.com/WileyCDA/

Books

Currently there are no books that solely explore the concept of the community college baccalaureate however there are some that touch on the subject.

Cohen, A. M., & Brawer, F. B. (2003). *The American community college*, 4th ed. San Francisco: Jossey-Bass.

Abstract: The American community college has become the primary resource that faculty, administrators, trustees, and researchers look to for a comprehensive analysis of the most recent findings and up-to-date information on the American community college. The authors describe how community colleges fit into the American educational system, the services they provide, and the effects they have on the community.

Dougherty, K. (1994). *The contradictory college: The conflict origins, impacts, and futures of the community college*. New York: SUNY Press.

Abstract: The author describes a variety of issues facing the American community college today. Dougherty begins with the importance of and controversy surrounding the community college. The author presents a debate of various topics like, reasons the community college was established, and the societal effects of the community college. A discussion of the impact of the community college on students, the economy, and the university follows. The origins and expansion of the community college is offered. Two aspects of structural reform are discussed; transforming community colleges into four year institutions and converting community colleges into state branches.

Levin, J. (2002). *Globalizing the community college: Strategies for change in the twenty-first century.* London: Palgrave Macmillan Press.

Abstract: The information presented in this book is from a comparative study of the influences of globalization and globalizing trends on community colleges in the United States and Canada (data collected from 1996 to 1999). Levin, explores seven community colleges that have undergone organizational change in response to globalization and discusses the effects in the economic, cultural, and information domains. The author presents both the both pros and cons.

Canada

To date there have been relatively few published documents relating to the community college baccalaureate in Canada. The publications that do exist pertain to the establishment and experience of the university colleges in British Columbia. In Alberta and Ontario there have been no publications relating to the applied baccalaureate. The approval processes for community college baccalaureates in Alberta and Ontario are highly centralized, and the Web sites of the provincial agencies that oversee these processes contain useful information about both the approval processes and the programs that have been approved. Besides those Web sites, there are a few published articles about the university colleges in British Columbia and a few conference papers about the applied baccalaureate degrees in Ontario. No doctoral dissertations about the community college baccalaureate have yet been completed, but several are now under way in the Community College Leadership

Program in the University of Toronto. Recently, the subject has been attracting considerable attention.

Web Sites

Alberta Learning: www.learning.gov.ab.ca/college/AppliedDegree

Alberta Learning is the name of the provincial ministry that oversees the process under which community colleges and technical institutes obtain approval for and offer applied baccalaureate degree programs. The Web site describes the history of the applied degrees in Alberta, which dates back to a pilot project in 1995–96, outlines the approval process, and lists all programs currently being offered. There is also an informative section of Frequently Asked Questions that states quite emphatically that offering applied baccalaureates is not a step to becoming a university.

Contact Information:
Alberta Learning
7th floor, Commerce Place
10155-102 Street
Edmonton, Alberta T5J 4L5
Phone: 780.427.7219
Fax: 780.422.1263
www.learning.gov.ab.ca

Association of Canadian Community Colleges: www.accc.ca

The association's Web site contains a listing of member institutions, information about Canadian community colleges, research, publications, conferences, and job opportunities. It also publishes a newsmagazine about developments in Canada's community colleges entitled *College Canada.*

Contact information:
Association of Canadian Community Colleges
200-1223 Michael Street North
Ottawa, Ontario K1J 7T2
Phone: 613.746.2222
Fax: 613.746.6721
www.accc.ca

Degree Quality Assessment Board: www.aved.gov.bc.ca/degree-authorization/

This is a recently established agency in British Columbia (BC) with responsibilities somewhat similar to those of the Postsecondary Education Quality Assessment Board (PEQAB) in Ontario. The BC board reviews the quality and makes recommendations to the minister of Advanced Education regarding degree-program proposals of private and out-of-province institutions and program proposals for applied baccalaureate degrees of British Columbia community colleges and technical institutes. The Web site provides information on the application process and will list all applications but displayed none as of December 2003.

Contact information:
Degree Quality Assessment Board
Ministry of Advanced Education
P.O. Box 9177, Stn Prov Govt
Victoria, B.C. V8W 9H8
Phone: 250.387.5163
www.aved.gov.bc.ca/degree-authorization/

Postsecondary Education Quality Assessment Board (PEQAB): www.peqab.edu.gov.on.ca

The PEQAB conducts institutional and program reviews and makes recommendations to the Ontario Ministry of Training, Colleges and Universities concerning applications for ministerial consent to offer degree programs in Ontario. Its purview includes private degree-granting institutions in Ontario, out-of-province universities seeking to offer degree programs in Ontario, and Ontario colleges of applied arts and technology (CAATs) seeking to offer applied baccalaureate degree programs. The Web site provides detailed information on the application process and standards for the community college applied baccalaureate programs and all other degree programs. The Web site also lists all programs for which applications have been made and indicates those that have received approval from the minister. Further, it is possible to view colleges' applications to offer applied baccalaureate programs, some as long as 200 pages.

Contact information:
Postsecondary Education Quality Assessment Board
9th floor, Mowat Block
900 Bay Street
Toronto, Ontario M7A 1L2
Phone: 416.325.1886
Fax: 316.325.1711
www.peqab.edu.gov.on.ca

Journals

The Canadian Journal of Higher Education: Published by the Canadian Society for the Study of Higher Education, Canada's premier scholarly journal on higher education covers community colleges. Its principal focus is Canadian, but it includes findings of research in other countries as well.

Dennison, J. D. (1992). The university college idea: A critical analysis. *Canadian Journal of Higher Education, 22*(1), pp. 109–124.

Abstract: The author discusses the history of and rationale for the conversion of some British Columbia community colleges into university colleges, institutions that incorporate the mandate of the community college with baccalaureate programming. The article contains an insightful discussion of the problems and issues involved in attempting to create a hybrid institution.

Contact information:
Canadian Journal of Higher Education
Centre for Higher Education Research and Development
University of Manitoba
220 Sinnott Building
70 Dysart Road
Winnipeg, Manitoba R3T 2N2
Phone: 204.474.6211
Fax: 204.474.7607
www.education.mcgill.ca/csshe

College Quarterly: www.collegequarterly.ca
    The *College Quarterly* is the only journal in Canada devoted exclusively to community colleges. It is intended primarily for college educators;

it emphasizes reporting on recent developments and research findings and encourages dialogue on issues in colleges, particularly related to the improvement of education. In recent years, there have been several articles pertaining to relations between community colleges and universities.

Contact information:
College Quarterly
Seneca College of Applied Arts and Technology
1750 Finch Avenue East
Toronto, Ontario M2J 2X5
Phone: 416.491.5050, Ex. 2080
Fax: 416.491.7745
www.collegequarterly.ca

CCBA Beacon: The *CCBA Beacon* provides information on developments regarding the community college baccalaureate in Canada as well as the United States (and other countries also). Aside from the article below, there have been brief news reports about developments in Canada. Resource:

Carr, B. (Winter 2001). The university college system in British Columbia, Canada. *CCBA Beacon, 2*(1), pp. 2–7.

Abstract: This article traces the development of the university colleges in British Columbia, starting with the historical context and the government's rationale for converting three community colleges into hybrid institutions. It then describes the experience of these three university colleges and two subsequent creations and discusses current challenges.

Contact information:
Community College Baccalaureate Association
P.O. Box 60210
Ft. Myers, FL 33906
Phone: 239.489.9295
Fax: 239.489.9250
www.accbd.org/

Policy Papers

Orton, L. (November 2003). *A new understanding of postsecondary education in Canada: A discussion paper.* Ottawa: Statistics Canada. Catalogue No. 81-595-MIE, n11.

Abstract: This paper describes problems in the present classification system for postsecondary education used by Statistics Canada, the national data-collection and -reporting agency, resulting from changes in postsecondary education over the past two decades, and proposes substantial revisions. One of the major educational changes considered is the provision of baccalaureate degree programs by community colleges, and the paper discusses how to reflect this new development in the classification system. The paper can be downloaded from the Statistics Canada Web site: www.statcan.ca/cgi-bin/downpub/listpub.cgi?catno=81-595-MIE2003011

Skolnik, M. L. (1999). *CAATs, universities, and degrees: Towards some options for enhancing the connection between CAATs and degrees.* A discussion paper prepared for the Ontario College-University Consortium Council. Toronto: CUCC.

Abstract: This paper was commissioned by the College-University Consortium Council (CUCC), an agency whose mandate is to foster improved coordination and collaboration between the two sectors of Ontario postsecondary education. The paper analyzes the problems caused by the lack of opportunities for community college students to continue on to completion of a baccalaureate degree and discusses options for improving the situation, including enabling the colleges to offer baccalaureate programs. The paper provided the basis for a historic meeting between officials of the two sectors that resulted in a province-wide agreement on articulation. The paper is available on the CUCC's Web site: www.cou.on.ca.cucc

Conference Papers

Skolnik, M. L. (February 18, 2002). *The CAATs and change: Is there an essence that has remained constant? Does it matter? The 2002 Sisco Address.* Annual Conference of the Association of Colleges of Applied Arts and Technology of Ontario, London, Ontario.

Abstract: This paper describes the changes that Ontario community colleges have experienced since their founding in 1967, including particularly the adoption of the community college baccalaureate degree and generally increased provision of university credit courses. It then reflects on the question of whether these types of changes are consistent with the mandate of the community college or whether the essence of community college has been changed. The paper is available on the Web site of the Association of Colleges of Applied Arts and Technology of Ontario: www.acaato.on.ca/

Skolnik, M. L. (February 7–9, 2001). *The community college baccalaureate: Its meaning and implications for the organization of postsecondary education, the mission and character of the community college, and the bachelor's degree.* Paper presented at the First Annual Community College Baccalaureate Association Conference: Learning from the Past, Shaping the Future, Orlando, FL.

Abstract: This paper discusses how the adoption of the baccalaureate degree by community colleges can change the structure of postsecondary education, and also what this development might imply for the meaning of a baccalaureate degree. In the discussion the author contrasts the situations in the United States and in Canada. The paper is available on the author's Web site in the faculty section of the Web site for the University of Toronto Doctoral Program in Community College Leadership: www.clix.to/cohortians

Book Chapters

Dennison, J. D. (1997). Higher education in British Columbia. In G. A. Jones (Ed.), *Higher education in Canada: Different systems, different perspectives* (pp. 31–58). New York: Garland Publishing, Inc.

Abstract: The author traces the evolution of higher education in British Columbia, showing how the establishment of university colleges fit in the historical development of higher education in the province. The chapter also identifies major issues in higher education in British Columbia, including questions about the changing role of community colleges.

BIOGRAPHIES OF AUTHORS AND EDITORS

Michelle Eastham is a doctoral candidate at the University of California–Los Angeles. Her dissertation is focused on the American community college baccalaureate. Specifically, she is examining the organizational changes a community college endures when deciding to offer baccalaureate degrees.

Deborah L. Floyd is an Associate Professor of Higher Education Leadership at Florida Atlantic University in Boca Raton. She has over twenty-five years of administrative experience in community colleges as a president, vice president, dean, and director, and has served on numerous national boards including the Board of Directors of the American Association of Community Colleges (AACC). Her publications and consultations are in areas of leadership, policy and governance, curriculum, community colleges, and student affairs.

Thomas E. Furlong, Jr. is the Senior Vice President for Baccalaureate Programs and University Partnership at St. Petersburg College in Florida. He has served as the Chief Academic Affairs Officer of the Florida Community College System, Executive Director of the Florida Postsecondary Education Planning Commission and as Vice President of Educational Services at Tallahassee Community College.

Berta Vigil Laden is a former community college faculty member and administrator. She is currently serving as an Associate Professor of Theory and Policy Studies with the Ontario Institute for Studies in Education of the University of Toronto, Ontario. Her research interests are in areas of community colleges, especially focusing on equity and retention of underrepresented students is higher education.

Albert L. Lorenzo is President of Macomb Community College in Michigan. He and his college have a reputation for programmatic innovations, including one of the nation's most successful University Centers. His previous publications have focused on leadership, planning and organizational development, and he currently serves on the Michigan Governor's Council of Economic Advisors.

Jonathon V. McKee is the Community College Director of the Washington State University, Vancouver, Engineering and Science Institute—a partnership of two community colleges and the university that delivers bachelor's degrees in Mechanical Engineering, Computer Science and Biology. He is also the Vocational Director at Clark College in Vancouver, Washington, where among other duties he oversees the Bachelor of Science degrees in Dental Hygiene and Advanced Technology.

Mark David Milliron is president and CEO of the League for Innovation in the Community College, an international consortium of more than seven hundred and fifty institutions from 15 different countries. As an author, speaker, and consultant, he has worked with colleges, corporations, and governments across the country and around the world. He has served on the board of the American Council on Education (ACE) and sits on several other educational, nonprofit, and corporate boards.

Nancy Remington is a Ph.D. candidate at the University of Nevada–Reno and formerly the lead faculty for the Elementary Education Baccalaureate Degree program at Great Basin College in Nevada. Her 30-year teaching experience spans the spectrum of education including preschool, primary, elementary, middle and high school, and three of Nevada's community colleges.

Ronald K. Remington has over thirty-five years of experience as a faculty member and administrator in higher education and has served during the past 15 years as president of two Nevada community colleges. During his 12-year presidency at Great Basin College he pioneered innovative baccalaureate degree programs in Elementary Education, Applied Sciences, and Integrative and Professional Studies. Under his leadership, the Community College of Southern Nevada stands poised to offer its first baccalaureate degree in dental hygiene.

Michael L. Skolnik is a Professor of Higher Education and the William G. Davis Chair in Community College Leadership at the Ontario Institute for Studies in Education of the University of Toronto. He is also a member of the Postsecondary Education Quality Assessment Board, a government appointed board which assesses proposed degree programs of community colleges and private and out-of-province universities. His publications include more than seventy books, monographs, and articles on higher education and he has served as an editor of the *Canadian Journal of Higher Education.*

Barbara K. Townsend is Professor of Higher Education at the University of Missouri–Columbia and a former community college faculty member and administrator. She is a former Executive Director of the Association for the Study of Higher Education (ASHE) and a past president of the Council for the Study of Community Colleges (CSCC).

Kenneth P. Walker is the founder of the Community College Baccalaureate Association (CCBA) and the Chairman of the CCBA Board of Directors. During his 42 years of teaching and leadership experience in community colleges—with 30 as a president—he has been a leader in providing access to the baccalaureate. He is currently the District President of Edison College in Ft. Myers, Florida. His publications include over twenty articles, many of which are on topics related to access and the community college baccalaureate.